I0013493

Networking for Beginners

Understanding the Internet and IT Infrastructure A practical guide to how the internet, IP addresses, and networking work

THOMPSON CARTER

Table of Content

TABLE OF CONTENTS

Introduction

Networking for Beginners: Understanding the Internet and IT Infrastructure

In today's fast-paced digital world, networking is at the core of almost every technology we interact with on a daily basis. Whether you're browsing the internet, sending emails, using cloud storage, or connecting to a Wi-Fi network, networking technology plays an essential role in enabling these interactions. For individuals and businesses alike, understanding how networking works is crucial for ensuring smooth and efficient operations in the ever-evolving landscape of technology.

This book, **"Networking for Beginners: Understanding the Internet and IT Infrastructure,"** serves as an accessible guide to help you build a solid foundation in networking concepts and technologies. Designed for both beginners and those who want to brush up on their networking knowledge, this book aims to simplify complex topics, break down jargon, and provide you with practical insights into how modern networks are designed, managed, and optimized.

Why Networking Matters

In a world where **communication** and **data transfer** are vital to business success and personal convenience, networking has become a critical skill. Whether you're setting up a home network, securing a business's internal systems, or working with cloud services, understanding the principles of networking helps you troubleshoot problems, optimize your systems, and ensure the reliability of your internet and local networks.

Networking affects various aspects of our daily digital experience:

- **Business Connectivity**: Companies rely on well-designed networks to facilitate communication between departments, enable collaboration, and run essential business applications like customer relationship management (CRM) and enterprise resource planning (ERP).
- **Internet Access**: Whether it's via a home broadband connection, a mobile hotspot, or an office network,

knowing how to optimize your internet connection or troubleshoot issues is more important than ever.

- **Security**: In an age where data breaches and cyber threats are frequent, networking knowledge is key to protecting sensitive information and ensuring the integrity of systems.
- **Cloud and Remote Work**: With the rise of cloud computing and remote work, understanding cloud networking and how to connect to remote servers is indispensable.

What You Will Learn

This book covers everything from the basic principles of networking to advanced concepts, providing an easy-to-understand guide for navigating the digital world. You will gain a solid understanding of key networking components, technologies, and protocols, as well as practical applications in the context of modern IT infrastructures. Here's a glimpse of what you can expect to learn:

1. **Foundations of Networking**: Learn the basic concepts behind **IP addresses**, **subnets**, and **DNS**— the building blocks of any network.

2. **Network Devices and Hardware**: Get acquainted with common networking devices, such as **routers**, **switches**, and **modems**, and understand their roles in both local area networks (LANs) and wide area networks (WANs).

3. **Internet and Communication Protocols**: Understand how the **internet** works, including the **OSI model**, **TCP/IP protocols**, and key technologies like **HTTP, FTP**, and **DNS**.

4. **Wi-Fi, Ethernet, and Other Connectivity Options**: Learn how different types of connections—**Wi-Fi**, **Ethernet**, and **cellular networks**—work to connect devices across short and long distances.

5. **Security and Protection**: Explore the importance of securing your network through **firewalls, VPNs**, and **intrusion detection systems** (IDS), while understanding common **cybersecurity threats**.

6. **Cloud Networking**: Understand how modern businesses leverage the **cloud** for scalability and efficiency, and how networks are set up to support cloud services.

7. **Network Troubleshooting**: Learn how to diagnose and fix common networking issues, from slow

connections to device conflicts, ensuring that your
network runs smoothly.

8. **Emerging Trends in Networking**: Get a glimpse of
the **future of networking**, including advancements
like **5G**, **AI in networking**, and how these will
transform industries and everyday life.

How This Book Is Structured

Each chapter of this book is carefully designed to build upon
the knowledge of the previous one, so you can progress step-
by-step as you deepen your understanding of networking.
The content is broken down into clear, digestible sections,
with real-world examples and practical applications that
make the abstract concepts more relatable.

Additionally, each chapter concludes with a summary and a
list of key takeaways to reinforce what you've learned. The
examples and scenarios used throughout the book will help
you see how these concepts play out in everyday situations,
providing a direct connection between theory and real-life
use.

Who Should Read This Book?

This book is ideal for anyone looking to understand the fundamentals of networking. Whether you're:

- A **beginner** looking to learn about networking from the ground up
- A **student** or aspiring IT professional aiming to build a career in networking or IT infrastructure
- An **entrepreneur** or **business owner** who wants to optimize and secure their company's network
- A **home user** wanting to troubleshoot slow internet connections or set up a more secure home network

This book is tailored to your needs and provides the foundational knowledge necessary to take your understanding of networking to the next level.

A Future-Proof Skill

As businesses and technologies evolve, the need for reliable, secure, and efficient networks will continue to grow. Whether it's for personal use or within a corporate environment, understanding networking will give you the tools to manage, optimize, and protect networks now and in the future. From small home networks to massive enterprise infrastructures, networking is a skill that's indispensable in the digital age.

Welcome to **"Networking for Beginners: Understanding the Internet and IT Infrastructure"**—a comprehensive guide to mastering the essentials of networking and setting yourself up for success in the connected world. Whether you're just getting started or looking to refresh your knowledge, this book is your first step toward becoming a confident and skilled network user. Let's dive in and explore the dynamic world of networking!

Part 1

Introduction to Networking and IT Infrastructure

CHAPTER 1

INTRODUCTION TO NETWORKING

What is Networking?

At its core, **networking** refers to the process of connecting multiple devices so they can share information and resources. It involves the communication between devices—such as computers, smartphones, printers, or servers—using both hardware (like cables, routers, and switches) and software (like protocols, applications, and services).

Networking can take many forms depending on its purpose and scale, from a simple home network that connects a few devices, to large-scale enterprise networks that handle millions of devices and vast amounts of data.

Networking isn't just about the physical connections; it's also about how information is sent, received, and processed. To make this happen, networking relies on a set of **protocols**, which are like rules that help devices "speak the same language" to ensure smooth communication. These protocols cover everything from the low-level details of how data is transmitted to how websites are accessed.

14

Overview of Networking in Daily Life

In today's world, networking is embedded in almost everything we do, often without us even realizing it. It plays a vital role in how we communicate, work, learn, and entertain ourselves. Every time you browse the web, send an email, or stream a video, you're interacting with networks—whether it's the internet, a local network at work, or a mobile network that connects you while you're on the go.

Here's how networking impacts daily life:

- **Home Networking**: Your home network is an example of a simple local network that connects your computers, smartphones, tablets, smart TVs, and other devices. These devices use your router to connect to the internet, share files, stream media, and even control smart home devices like thermostats and security cameras.

- **Office Networks**: In an office setting, networking allows employees to share files, communicate with each other, access resources like printers and servers, and connect to the internet. An office network might be more complex than a home network, with security measures in place to protect sensitive data and separate networks for different departments.

- **Public Wi-Fi**: Public networks, like those in coffee shops, airports, or libraries, let users access the internet from their devices. These networks are often less secure than private networks, which is why it's important to be cautious when using them to access personal or financial information.

Real-World Examples

1. **Home   Networks**:
   Imagine you're at home, and you want to connect your laptop to the internet. You turn on your router, which acts as a central hub to distribute your internet connection to all your devices—whether they are connected through Wi-Fi or Ethernet cables. You use your home network to check your email, watch YouTube, or print a document.

2. **Office   Networks**:
   At work, you connect your computer to a corporate network through Ethernet or Wi-Fi. This network not only provides access to the internet, but it also lets you communicate with other employees through email and chat apps, access shared drives where files

are stored, and print documents to a shared printer. Larger companies often have more complex networks with additional layers of security and segmentation to protect sensitive data.

3. **Public   Wi-Fi**: When you visit a coffee shop, you can connect to their public Wi-Fi network to check your emails or browse the internet. This network is usually open or requires a simple login to access. However, because public networks are not as secure, it's important to avoid sensitive activities like online banking or entering passwords when connected to them.

In this chapter, we've laid the foundation for understanding what networking is and how it plays a role in everyday activities. Whether at home, in the office, or on the go, networking is at the heart of how devices communicate and share information. The next chapters will dive deeper into the specifics of networking devices, protocols, and the underlying structure that enables this connectivity.

CHAPTER 2

UNDERSTANDING THE INTERNET

What is the Internet?

The **internet** is a vast global network that connects millions of private, public, academic, business, and government devices worldwide. It allows for the exchange of data and information between these devices through a system of interconnected networks. The internet is essentially a network of networks, meaning that smaller networks (like those in homes or offices) are linked together to form a larger, more complex system that spans the entire globe.

At the core of the internet is a system of **protocols**—rules and standards that enable devices to communicate with one another. These protocols, such as the **Transmission Control Protocol** (TCP) and **Internet Protocol** (IP), are the foundation of how data is transferred from one device to another over the internet.

The internet serves as the backbone of nearly every online activity today, from browsing websites and checking emails to streaming videos and communicating with others across the globe.

How the Internet Connects the World

The internet works by connecting devices through various types of physical infrastructure, including **cables, satellites, cell towers,** and **fiber-optic lines**. Here's a breakdown of how these connections come together to form the internet:

1. **Internet Service Providers (ISPs)**: To access the internet, individuals and businesses connect to the internet via an ISP, which provides the necessary infrastructure and bandwidth. ISPs offer various types of connections, such as broadband, fiber-optic, or even satellite connections, to enable users to get online.

2. **Data Transmission**: Once you're connected to the internet, data travels in small packets from your device through routers and switches. These packets carry information such as the website you're visiting or the message you're sending. Routers help direct the packets to their destination by using the IP address associated with each device or website.

3. **The Role of Servers**: The internet relies on **servers**, which are specialized computers that store information (such as website files, videos, and emails) and respond to requests from other computers. When you access a website or download a file, the server sends the requested data to your device over the internet.

4. **Global Connectivity**: The internet is built on a system of **backbones**—high-capacity data routes that carry large amounts of traffic between countries and continents. These backbones are connected by fiber-optic cables that stretch across the ocean floor and through the air via satellite connections, ensuring global connectivity.

Real-World Example: A Web Search Request

Let's break down a real-world scenario where you perform a **web search**. Imagine you want to search for "best restaurants in New York" using your smartphone.

1. **You type the search query into a search engine** (e.g., Google).

2. **Your device sends a request to the search engine's server**. This request travels over the internet, passing

through several routers and switches, each of which determines the best path for the data.

3. The **search engine server receives your request** and looks up the information in its database. The server processes the query and prepares a response with the relevant results.

4. The search engine's response (which may include a list of websites, images, or other resources) is **broken into small data packets** and sent back to your device. These packets travel over the same network infrastructure and are reassembled once they reach your device.

5. **The results appear on your screen** in a matter of seconds, allowing you to explore various websites and find the information you're looking for.

In this example, the process may seem quick, but it involves multiple steps and complex interactions between various devices, servers, and networks, all working together seamlessly to get the information to your device.

In this chapter, we've explored the internet's definition and how it connects the world. We've also looked at a real-world example of a web search request, which helps illustrate how data moves across the internet from one point to another. As we move forward, we'll dive deeper into how networking protocols, servers, and devices work together to make this all possible.

CHAPTER 3

THE BASICS OF IT INFRASTRUCTURE

What is IT Infrastructure?

IT infrastructure refers to the collection of physical and virtual resources needed to support the operation of information technology (IT) systems. It includes both hardware and software components that enable the functioning of networks, data storage, security, and applications within an organization.

IT infrastructure is the backbone that supports all digital activities in a business or home network. Without it, devices and systems would not be able to communicate with each other, access data, or run applications. The infrastructure is designed to ensure that the IT environment is stable, secure, and scalable to meet the growing needs of users and organizations.

In general, IT infrastructure includes:

- **Hardware**: The physical devices like computers, servers, routers, and storage devices that make up the network.

- **Software**: The applications, operating systems, and network management tools that help control and manage hardware resources.
- **Networking Components**: Routers, switches, firewalls, and cables that connect devices to each other and to the internet.
- **Data Storage**: Systems for storing and retrieving data, such as databases, file servers, or cloud storage.
- **Security**: Tools and protocols for protecting the network and data, including firewalls, encryption, antivirus software, and access controls.

The Role of Hardware and Software

Both **hardware** and **software** play crucial roles in IT infrastructure, and they work together to ensure the proper functioning of a network or system.

1. **Hardware**:
   Hardware forms the physical layer of IT infrastructure. It includes devices like:
   - **Servers**: Powerful computers that store data, run applications, and provide services to other devices (clients).
   - **Routers and Switches**: Devices that manage data traffic, directing it where it needs to go within the network or to the internet.

24

- o **Workstations and End-User Devices**: Computers, laptops, mobile phones, and other devices that interact with the network and access services.
- o **Storage Devices**: Hard drives, solid-state drives (SSDs), and network-attached storage (NAS) systems that store data.

2. **Software**:

Software manages and controls the hardware. It provides the interface and functionality needed for users to interact with devices and networks. Key software components include:

- o **Operating Systems (OS)**: Software that allows hardware to interact with users and applications. Examples include Windows, macOS, Linux, and Android.
- o **Networking Software**: Tools that manage and configure network devices, ensuring smooth communication across the infrastructure (e.g., firewalls, VPNs, network monitoring tools).
- o **Applications**: Programs that run on the network and provide specific services, such as email, word processing, web browsing, and database management.

The combination of reliable hardware and efficient software is essential for a stable, secure, and scalable IT infrastructure. It allows businesses to operate smoothly, employees to be productive, and systems to communicate and share data.

Real-World Example: Setting Up an Office Network

Let's consider the process of setting up a basic office network for a small business. Here's how the IT infrastructure components come together:

1. **Planning the Network Layout**:
   o The first step is to determine the office layout and the number of devices that will be connected. This includes deciding on the number of computers, printers, phones, and other devices that need to communicate.
   o The network architect will plan where to place routers, switches, and wireless access points to ensure coverage across the office.
2. **Installing Networking Hardware**:
   o A **router** is installed to provide internet access and connect the office network to the outside world. The router acts as the gateway for all internet traffic.

26

- o **Switches** are added to connect various devices within the office, like computers and printers. Switches allow data to flow between devices without the need for each device to directly connect to the router.
- o **Wi-Fi access points** are set up to allow wireless devices, such as laptops or smartphones, to connect to the network without the need for physical cables.

3. **Configuring Network Devices**:

- o The devices are connected to the network via **Ethernet cables** or Wi-Fi. Each device is assigned an **IP address** to ensure proper communication.
- o The router is configured with security settings like **firewalls** to protect the network from external threats. VPNs or secure Wi-Fi protocols (e.g., WPA2) are used to protect data traveling over the network.

4. **Installing and Setting Up Servers**:

- o A **server** is set up to handle various business functions, such as file sharing, email, and printing. A **file server** might be installed to store company documents, while an **email server** is used to manage communications between employees.

27

- o Software such as an **operating system** (e.g., Windows Server or Linux) is installed to manage the server's hardware and support various applications.

5. **Ensuring Network Security**:
   - o Security measures, such as antivirus software, **firewalls**, and access controls, are put in place to protect sensitive business data from cyber threats.
   - o A **network monitoring tool** might also be installed to track network performance and identify potential issues before they disrupt operations.

6. **Connecting Workstations**:
   - o Employees are provided with workstations (computers or laptops), which are connected to the network. They access shared drives, print documents, and communicate using applications hosted on the server.
   - o The devices are all set up with necessary software, such as email clients, office productivity tools, and web browsers.

By the end of the setup, the business has a functional office network that enables seamless communication, collaboration, and access to resources. The network infrastructure is designed to support day-to-day operations, with room for future expansion as the business grows.

In this chapter, we've introduced the fundamental components of IT infrastructure and explained the crucial roles of both hardware and software. The real-world example of setting up an office network provides a practical understanding of how these elements come together to support a functioning network. As we continue, we'll explore more advanced networking concepts that allow businesses to scale and secure their IT environments.

You said:

1. Key Networking Devices o Routers, switches, hubs, and modems. o How they function and their real-world applications. o Real-world example: How a router connects you to the internet.

ChatGPT said:

Chapter 4: Key Networking Devices

Routers, Switches, Hubs, and Modems

In any network, certain devices are crucial for ensuring smooth communication between devices and maintaining connectivity to the broader network or internet. The four most common types of networking devices are **routers**, **switches**, **hubs**, and **modems**. Let's break each one down:

1. **Routers**:

    A **router** is a device that connects different networks together and forwards data between them. For example, it connects your home or office network to the internet. The router uses **IP addresses** to direct the data to its proper destination. If you send an email or access a website, the router determines the best path for that data to travel across various networks and reaches the appropriate server or device.

    Function:

    o   Routes data between different networks.

    o   Assigns local IP addresses to devices on the network.

    o   Provides network security, usually with built-in firewalls to protect from external threats.

    o   Offers wireless connectivity (in many cases) for devices like laptops, phones, and smart devices.

2. **Switches**:

    A **switch** is a device that connects multiple devices within the same network, such as computers, printers, or servers. Unlike a hub (which broadcasts data to all connected devices), a switch intelligently forwards data only to the device that needs it. This helps improve network efficiency and reduces unnecessary traffic.

Function:

- o Connects devices within a local area network (LAN).
- o Directs data only to the device that requested it, improving efficiency.
- o Can operate at higher speeds, supporting more devices and larger data traffic.

3. **Hubs**:

A **hub** is a basic networking device that also connects devices within a network, but unlike a switch, it **broadcasts** data to all devices connected to it. This means that every device on the network receives the data, even if it wasn't the intended recipient. Hubs are outdated compared to switches, which are more efficient.

Function:

- o Sends data to all devices within a local network.

o Simple and inexpensive, but less efficient and secure than switches.

4. **Modems**:

A **modem** (short for **modulator-demodulator**) is a device that connects a local network (such as your home network) to the internet via an internet service provider (ISP). The modem converts digital signals from the local network into analog signals that can travel over telephone lines, cable, or fiber-optic connections, and vice versa. Essentially, the modem makes it possible to connect to the internet by translating between the local network and the ISP's infrastructure.

Function:

o Converts digital signals into analog signals and vice versa for internet access.
o Provides a connection between the local network and the ISP.
o Can be combined with a router in many modern devices (known as a gateway).

How They Function and Their Real-World Applications

Now let's look at how these devices function in real-world scenarios and how they work together in a network:

1. **Routers**: Routers are essential for connecting different networks. In a home network, for instance, the router connects the local area network (LAN)— which includes your computer, smartphone, and printer—to the **internet**, the wide-area network (WAN). The router handles assigning IP addresses to each device and ensures data is sent to and received from the right destination. Additionally, routers often come with built-in **Wi-Fi**, allowing wireless devices to connect.

2. **Switches**: In a medium or large office, multiple devices need to communicate with one another. A **switch** is used to connect computers, printers, and servers within the same building or office. If someone sends a print job from their computer, the switch ensures that the data goes directly to the printer, without wasting bandwidth or slowing down the network by broadcasting to every device.

3. **Hubs**: Hubs used to be the go-to device for small networks, but now they are less common. They're

often found in very small or older networks where data traffic is light. They can connect devices like printers, computers, and cameras in a small home office, though their lack of efficiency and security means they're rarely used in modern setups.

4. **Modems**: A modem is used to connect your home network to your ISP's internet service. If you've ever had to set up your internet at home, you've likely interacted with a modem. The modem receives data from the ISP, converting it into a digital format your devices can understand. In many cases, **modem-router combos** are used, combining both modem and router functionality in one device for simplicity and convenience.

Real-World Example: How a Router Connects You to the Internet

Let's walk through a real-world example of how a **router** connects your home network to the internet.

1. **Connecting   to   the   Internet**: You receive your internet service from an ISP, and the ISP provides you with a **modem** that connects to their network. The modem is connected to a **router**

(either via Ethernet or as a combined modem-router device).

2. **Assigning IP Addresses**: When you turn on your router, it assigns an **IP address** to each device on your local network. This could be a laptop, smartphone, or smart TV. The router also uses **Network Address Translation (NAT)** to map the private IP addresses on your network to a public IP address assigned by your ISP.

3. **Sending Data**: You open your laptop and try to access a website. Your laptop sends a request to the router, which forwards that request to the modem. The modem sends it over the internet to the appropriate web server. The server processes your request, and the data (the website) travels back through the internet to the modem.

4. **Receiving Data**: The modem sends the data back to the router, which then directs it to the appropriate device (in this case, your laptop). The router uses the assigned IP address to ensure that the data goes to the correct device. The webpage appears on your laptop's browser.

In this example, the router is essential for both routing data between your local network and the internet and providing the functionality to allow devices on the network to communicate with one another.

In this chapter, we've covered the primary networking devices—routers, switches, hubs, and modems—and explained their functions and applications. These devices play key roles in establishing and maintaining networks, whether in a home, office, or large-scale enterprise. Understanding how they work together is crucial for setting up and managing an efficient and secure network.

CHAPTER 5

IP ADDRESSES AND THEIR IMPORTANCE

What is an IP Address?

An **IP address** (Internet Protocol address) is a unique identifier assigned to every device connected to a network, such as a computer, smartphone, or printer. Think of it as a "home address" for a device on the internet or within a local network. When data is transmitted over the network, the IP address tells the system where to send that data.

An IP address allows devices to locate and communicate with each other across different networks. It can either be static (permanent) or dynamic (changing), depending on how the network is configured.

IP addresses are used in conjunction with **DNS (Domain Name System)**, which translates human-readable domain names (like www.google.com) into the IP addresses that the internet uses to locate the web server and deliver the data.

IPv4 vs IPv6

There are two versions of IP addresses in use today: **IPv4** and **IPv6**. Each version serves the same purpose but has different structures and capabilities.

1. **IPv4**:

   IPv4 is the most widely used version of IP addressing today. An IPv4 address is composed of **32 bits**, which are divided into four groups of eight bits (called octets). Each octet is represented by a number between 0 and 255, and the entire address looks something like this: **192.168.1.1**

   IPv4 allows for about **4.3 billion** unique IP addresses. While this seems like a lot, the growth of the internet and the proliferation of devices has led to IPv4 address exhaustion, where all available IPs are assigned.

2. **IPv6**:

   To address the limitations of IPv4, **IPv6** was introduced. IPv6 uses **128 bits** for the address, allowing for a virtually unlimited number of unique addresses (around **340 undecillion**—that's 340 followed by 36 zeros!). IPv6 addresses are written in hexadecimal format (using numbers and letters), and they look like this: **2001:0db8:85a3:0000:0000:8a2e:0370:7334**

IPv6 was designed to handle the ever-growing number of internet-connected devices and to provide more efficient routing and security features. While adoption of IPv6 is still ongoing, it is expected to gradually replace IPv4 over time as the need for more addresses continues to grow.

Real-World Example: How IP Addresses Route Data Across the Internet

Let's go through a real-world example of how **IP addresses** are used to route data across the internet.

1. **You Send a Request**: You're sitting at home, and you want to visit your favorite website, www.example.com. You type the URL into your browser and hit enter. The browser doesn't know how to reach "www.example.com" directly because it only understands IP addresses. So, it first sends a request to a **DNS server** to translate the domain name into an IP address.

2. **DNS Resolves the IP Address**: The DNS server looks up the domain name and finds the corresponding **IP address** of the web server hosting **www.example.com**—for instance, **192.168.1.1** (this is a simplified example; real web server IPs will differ). The DNS server then returns this IP address to your browser.

3. **Routing the Data**: With the IP address in hand, your browser sends a **data packet** to the **router** connected to your home network. The router checks its routing table, which tells it how to forward data to the next device on the path to the destination. In most cases, your router forwards the request to your **Internet Service Provider (ISP)**, which then sends the request over the larger internet infrastructure.

4. **Navigating Through Networks**: Along the way, the request passes through multiple **routers** and networks, each of which knows how to send the data to the correct destination based on the IP address. The routers at various points in the network determine the best path for the data to take, hopping from one router to another until it reaches the web server hosting www.example.com.

5. **Web   Server   Responds**:
Once the data reaches the server, the server looks up
the requested webpage and sends the data back in the
form of a data packet. This packet is addressed with
your **IP address**, so the server knows where to send
the response.

6. **Data   Returns   to   Your   Device**:
The data travels back across the internet, passing
through routers and networks, until it reaches your
router, which knows how to direct the data to your
device using its local IP address. Your browser then
receives the webpage, processes it, and displays the
content on your screen.

In this example, the **IP address** served as the key address,
guiding the data from your device to the web server and
back. It's the unique identifier that makes sure the data
reaches the right place, ensuring communication between
devices across vast distances on the internet.

In this chapter, we've explored what an **IP address** is, the
difference between **IPv4** and **IPv6**, and how IP addresses are
used to route data across the internet. Whether you're

browsing the web, sending an email, or using an app, understanding how IP addresses work helps you grasp the underlying technology that makes the internet function.

Part 2

The Building Blocks of Networking

CHAPTER 6

NETWORK TOPOLOGIES

Types of Network Topologies: Star, Bus, Ring, and Mesh

A **network topology** refers to the physical or logical layout of a network, specifically how devices are connected to each other. The topology of a network has a significant impact on its performance, scalability, and fault tolerance. Here are the four most common types of network topologies:

1. **Star**   **Topology**

   In a **star topology**, all devices are connected to a central device, typically a **switch** or **hub**. This central device acts as a mediator that manages communication between all the devices. The central device is the hub of the network, and each device is connected to it via individual cables.

   Advantages:

   - o   Easy to install and manage.
   - o   If one device fails, it does not affect the rest of the network.
   - o   Centralized management (easier to monitor and control).

44

Disadvantages:

- o   If the central device (e.g., the switch or hub) fails, the entire network is disrupted.
- o   Requires more cabling than some other topologies.

2. **Bus** **Topology**

In a **bus topology**, all devices are connected to a single central cable, often referred to as the **bus** or backbone. Data sent by any device travels along the bus and is received by all other devices, but only the device with the correct address processes it.

Advantages:

- o   Simple and cost-effective for small networks.
- o   Requires less cable than a star topology.

Disadvantages:

- o   Difficult to troubleshoot, especially if there is a failure in the backbone cable.
- o   Performance degrades as more devices are added.
- o   If the central cable fails, the entire network is affected.

3. **Ring** **Topology**

In a **ring topology**, each device is connected to two

45

other devices, forming a circular loop. Data travels in one direction (or sometimes two, in a **dual ring topology**) around the ring. Each device in the network acts as a repeater to help the signal travel along the ring.

Advantages:

- o Data transmission is relatively fast, as it travels in one direction.
- o No collision of data occurs, reducing network traffic.

Disadvantages:

- o If one device or cable fails, the entire network can be affected.
- o Difficult to troubleshoot and expand.
- o Adding or removing devices can disrupt the network.

4. **Mesh**   **Topology**

In a **mesh topology**, every device is connected to every other device. This means there are multiple paths for data to travel, which increases the reliability and redundancy of the network. Mesh topologies can be either **full mesh** (where every device is directly connected to every other device) or **partial mesh** (where only some devices are directly connected).

Advantages:

- o High redundancy and reliability. If one connection fails, there are alternative paths for the data.
- o Suitable for critical networks where uptime is paramount (e.g., data centers, hospitals).

Disadvantages:

- o Expensive to install and maintain due to the high number of connections.
- o Can become complex to manage, especially in large networks.

How to Choose a Topology for Different Needs

When selecting a network topology, it's essential to consider the size of the network, budget, required performance, scalability, and fault tolerance. Here's a guide to help you choose the right topology for different needs:

1. **Star** **Topology**:
Ideal for **small to medium-sized networks** where ease of installation, management, and maintenance are key considerations. Star topology is also great for **home networks** or **small office networks**, where failure of one device won't bring down the whole network, and the central device can easily be monitored and maintained.

2. **Bus** **Topology**:
Best suited for **small networks** with fewer devices and lower data traffic. It's cost-effective and simple to set up but should be avoided for larger networks due to performance issues and difficulty in troubleshooting.

3. **Ring** **Topology**:
Ring topology is often used in **specialized environments** like **token-ring networks** or where high-speed data transfer with minimal collision is needed. However, due to its vulnerability to network failure from a single point, it is less common in general-purpose networks today.

4. **Mesh** **Topology**:
A **full mesh topology** is used for highly critical systems where maximum uptime and redundancy are

needed, such as in **large enterprises**, **data centers**, or **telecommunications networks**. For most applications, a **partial mesh topology** can offer a good balance of reliability and cost-efficiency.

Real-World Example: Choosing a Topology for a Home Network

Let's consider the process of choosing the right topology for a typical **home network**.

1. **Determining the Network Needs**: In a home network, the primary needs are **easy internet access**, **connecting multiple devices** (computers, smartphones, smart TVs, printers), and a network that is **easy to manage** and **expand**.

2. **Why Star Topology Works Well**: The **star topology** is typically the best choice for a home network because it's simple and cost-effective. In a home, the router acts as the central device, and all other devices connect to it either via **Wi-Fi** or **Ethernet cables**. If one device fails, the others remain unaffected, and it's easy to monitor and troubleshoot. Additionally, many modern routers include features like **wireless access points** and

Ethernet ports, which makes star topology even more practical.

3. **Network Components**:

   o **Router**: The central device that connects the home network to the internet.

   o **Wi-Fi and Ethernet**: Devices like laptops, smartphones, and printers connect to the router wirelessly or through Ethernet cables.

   o **Switch**: If you need to connect more devices via Ethernet, you could use a switch to expand the number of available ports on the router.

4. **Alternative   Topologies**: A **bus topology** would be impractical in a home network due to the risk of performance issues as more devices are added. Similarly, a **ring topology** is not ideal because it's difficult to troubleshoot, and a failure in any device could take down the whole network. **Mesh topology**, while providing excellent redundancy, would be overkill for a simple home setup due to its complexity and cost.

In this chapter, we've discussed the different types of network topologies—**star, bus, ring**, and **mesh**—and how to choose the right topology based on network size, performance needs, and budget. For most home networks, **star topology** provides the best combination of simplicity, scalability, and reliability, making it an ideal choice for connecting devices and ensuring smooth internet access.

CHAPTER 7

UNDERSTANDING SUBNETS AND SUBNETTING

What is a Subnet?

A **subnet** (short for **subnetwork**) is a smaller, more manageable segment of a larger network. It allows network administrators to divide a large network into smaller, isolated sections, which helps with organization, security, and performance. Each subnet operates as a separate network within a larger system, but all subnets within the same network share the same **network address**.

Think of a subnet as a **neighborhood** within a **city**. While the city represents the larger network, the neighborhood represents a smaller subset of devices that are grouped together, making the entire city (network) easier to manage and organize.

The process of dividing a larger network into smaller subnets is called **subnetting**.

Why Use Subnets?

There are several key reasons to use subnets in a network:

- **Efficiency**: It reduces network congestion by allowing traffic to be confined to smaller sections of the network, rather than having all devices communicate with each other over one large network.

- **Security**: Subnetting can help improve security by isolating sensitive areas of the network. For example, you can separate the payroll system from other parts of the business network, limiting access to only those who need it.

- **Organization**: Subnets help organize the network better, making it easier to manage and maintain.

- **Better Use of IP Addresses**: Subnetting allows a more efficient allocation of available IP addresses, especially in cases where there is a shortage of IPs (such as with IPv4).

Basic Subnetting Explained

To understand subnetting, you need to grasp a few key concepts:

1. **IP Address Structure**: An **IP address** is composed of two parts: the **network portion** and the **host portion**. The network portion identifies which network the device belongs to, while the host portion identifies the specific device on that network.

   For example, in the IPv4 address **192.168.1.10**:

- o **Network portion**: 192.168.1 (identifies the network).
- o **Host portion**: 10 (identifies the device within that network).

2. **Subnet Mask**: A **subnet mask** is used to determine which part of the IP address refers to the network and which part refers to the host. It essentially "masks" the network portion of the address, allowing the network to be divided into smaller subnets.

   A typical subnet mask for a small network might look like this: **255.255.255.0**

   - o The **255** values in the subnet mask correspond to the **network portion** of the IP address.
   - o The **0** value corresponds to the **host portion**.

   This subnet mask tells the network that the first three octets (192.168.1) are the network portion, and the last octet (10) represents the host portion.

3. **CIDR Notation**: Instead of writing the subnet mask as a series of four octets (like 255.255.255.0), you can use **CIDR (Classless Inter-Domain Routing)** notation, which expresses the network size by the

number of bits used for the network portion. For example, **192.168.1.0/24** means that the first 24 bits of the IP address are used for the network portion, which is the same as the subnet mask **255.255.255.0**.

4. **Creating Subnets**: By borrowing bits from the host portion of the IP address, you can create subnets within the larger network. The more bits you borrow, the more subnets you can create, but the fewer host addresses each subnet will have.

For example, if you start with the IP address **192.168.1.0/24** and want to create two subnets, you could borrow one bit from the host portion, creating a new subnet mask of **255.255.255.128** (or **/25** in CIDR notation). This divides the original network into two subnets, each with a maximum of 126 host addresses.

Real-World Example: Breaking Down a Large Network into Smaller, Manageable Subnets

Let's say you have a large organization with several departments—**HR**, **Sales**, and **IT**—and you need to design a network that ensures each department has its own subnet, improving performance, security, and manageability.

55

1. **Step 1: Start with the Network Address**
   You are given the IP address **192.168.1.0/24**. This means the network address is **192.168.1.0**, and you have 256 possible IP addresses (0-255).

2. **Step 2: Decide How Many Subnets You Need**
   You want to create three subnets for the three departments: HR, Sales, and IT. Since **/24** gives you only one large network, you'll need to borrow bits from the host portion of the address to create subnets.

3. **Step 3: Subnet the Network**
   If you borrow two bits from the host portion, you'll get a subnet mask of **255.255.255.192** (or **/26** in CIDR notation). This allows you to create four subnets, each with 64 IP addresses (since 2 bits for the subnet gives you 4 subnets: $2^2 = 4$).

The new subnets will look like this:

- o Subnet 1: **192.168.1.0/26** (IP range: 192.168.1.0 to 192.168.1.63)
- o Subnet 2: **192.168.1.64/26** (IP range: 192.168.1.64 to 192.168.1.127)
- o Subnet 3: **192.168.1.128/26** (IP range: 192.168.1.128 to 192.168.1.191)

o Subnet 4: **192.168.1.192/26** (IP range: 192.168.1.192 to 192.168.1.255)

Each department (HR, Sales, IT) can now be assigned a subnet, and any extra subnets can be used for other purposes (e.g., for guest Wi-Fi or printers).

4. **Step 4: Assign IP Addresses to Devices**
Now that the network is segmented into subnets, you can assign IP addresses to devices in each department. For example:

   o HR might use IPs from **192.168.1.1** to **192.168.1.62**.
   o Sales might use IPs from **192.168.1.65** to **192.168.1.126**.
   o IT might use IPs from **192.168.1.129** to **192.168.1.190**.

5. **Step 5: Advantages of Subnetting**
   o **Improved Performance**: Traffic within each department's subnet stays local, reducing congestion.
   o **Enhanced Security**: Sensitive data in HR can be isolated from Sales and IT.
   o **Easier Management**: Devices are grouped based on their function, making the network easier to manage.

In this chapter, we've explained the concept of **subnets** and how **subnetting** works to break a larger network into smaller, more manageable sections. We also looked at a real-world example of how subnetting can be applied in an organization to segment the network for improved performance, security, and management. Understanding subnetting is a critical skill for anyone involved in network administration, as it allows for more efficient use of IP addresses and better network organization.

CHAPTER 8

THE OSI MODEL: LAYERS OF NETWORKING

Introduction to the OSI Model and Each Layer

The **OSI model** (Open Systems Interconnection model) is a conceptual framework that describes how data travels across a network. It divides the process of communication into **seven distinct layers**, each of which handles a specific aspect of the communication. The OSI model is essential for understanding how networks operate and troubleshooting network issues.

The seven layers of the OSI model, from bottom to top, are:

1. **Layer 1: Physical Layer**
   The **physical layer** is responsible for the actual transmission of raw data over physical media, such as cables, fiber optics, or wireless signals. This layer deals with hardware elements like network interface cards (NICs), switches, and routers. It defines the electrical, mechanical, and procedural aspects of physical communication.

Key Functions:

- o Transmission of bits (0s and 1s) over physical mediums.
- o Defines characteristics like voltage, pinouts, and cable types.

Real-world example: The copper wires or fiber-optic cables used to connect devices in a home or office network.

2. **Layer 2: Data Link Layer**

   The **data link layer** is responsible for error detection and correction, as well as the proper framing of data packets. It ensures that data is delivered without errors to the correct device on the network. This layer uses **MAC addresses** to identify devices on the same local network.

   Key Functions:

   - o Frames data for transmission.
   - o Handles error detection and correction at the bit level.
   - o Manages physical device addresses (MAC addresses).

Real-world example: Ethernet protocols are part of the data link layer and handle the addressing and error checking for devices within a local area network (LAN).

3. **Layer 3: Network Layer**
The **network layer** is responsible for routing data packets between devices across different networks. It uses **IP addresses** to identify source and destination devices. The network layer determines the optimal path for data transmission using routing protocols.

Key Functions:

- o Routes data packets between different networks.
- o Handles logical addressing (e.g., IP addresses).
- o Determines the best path for data to travel.

Real-world example: A **router** operates at this layer, forwarding data packets to their destination based on IP addresses.

4. **Layer 4: Transport Layer**
The **transport layer** ensures reliable data transmission between two devices on different networks. It manages data flow control, error

61

correction, and retransmission of lost data. The transport layer uses **port numbers** to direct data to the correct application.

Key Functions:

- o Provides end-to-end communication and error handling.
- o Ensures reliable data delivery using protocols like **TCP** and **UDP**.
- o Manages data flow control to prevent congestion.

Real-world example: The **TCP** (Transmission Control Protocol) ensures reliable communication when you load a webpage, ensuring all data is received and in the correct order.

5. **Layer 5: Session Layer**
The **session layer** manages and controls the communication sessions between devices. It ensures that data from different applications or services is kept separate, maintaining organized communication between applications.

Key Functions:

o Manages sessions between devices (establishing, maintaining, and terminating).

o Controls data exchange between applications.

o Ensures that communication sessions are synchronized.

Real-world example: A **video conferencing application** (like Zoom or Skype) uses the session layer to manage multiple sessions during a call, maintaining the communication between users.

6. **Layer 6: Presentation Layer**
The **presentation layer** is responsible for translating data into a format that can be understood by the application layer. This includes encryption, data compression, and converting data between different formats. It ensures that data is presented in a readable format.

Key Functions:

o Translates data from the application layer into a format suitable for transmission.

o Handles data encryption, decryption, and compression.

Real-world example: When you open a file on your computer, the **presentation layer** ensures the data is in the right format (like converting a text file into something your word processor can display).

7. **Layer 7: Application Layer**
The **application layer** is the closest layer to the end user. It provides the interface and services that allow applications to interact with the network. This layer includes web browsers, email clients, file transfer applications, and any other software that relies on network communication.

Key Functions:

o   Provides network services to applications (e.g., HTTP for web browsers, SMTP for email).

o   Facilitates communication between the user and the network.

Real-world example: When you send an email, the application layer (e.g., the email client like Outlook or Gmail) interfaces with the network to send the message.

Real-World Example: How Data Moves Through the Layers When Sending an Email

Let's take a real-world example of **sending an email** and break down how the data moves through the OSI layers:

1. **Layer 7 (Application Layer)**:
   - You compose an email using your email client (e.g., Outlook, Gmail). At this point, you're interacting with the application layer.
   - You hit **Send**, and the email client creates the data packet for transmission, ready to be sent to the destination server.

2. **Layer 6 (Presentation Layer)**:
   - The application layer hands the email data to the presentation layer, where it may be encoded or compressed (e.g., for attachments).
   - If the email is encrypted, this would happen at the presentation layer as well.

3. **Layer 5 (Session Layer)**:
   - The session layer ensures that the session between your device and the email server is set up and maintained. It manages the session for the duration of the email transmission.

4. **Layer 4 (Transport Layer)**:

o The email data is passed to the transport layer, where **TCP** or **UDP** ensures the reliable delivery of the email. The transport layer breaks the email into smaller data packets and attaches a port number to each one.

o The email client on your device communicates with the email server, ensuring the email is sent successfully.

5. **Layer 3 (Network Layer)**:

o The data packets are then passed to the network layer, where they are assigned an **IP address** (the source and destination addresses) to ensure they are routed correctly.

o Routers along the way use the IP address to route the packets through the internet to the email server.

6. **Layer 2 (Data Link Layer)**:

o As the email packets travel across networks, the data link layer handles the framing and error checking for the transmission. The data link layer also uses **MAC addresses** to ensure the data reaches the correct physical device on the local network.

7. **Layer 1 (Physical Layer)**:

o   Finally, the data is transmitted over physical media, whether through **Ethernet cables**, **Wi-Fi**, or **fiber-optic lines**.

o   The raw bits of data travel over these mediums, moving across network infrastructure toward the destination email server.

Once the data reaches the destination email server, it travels back through the layers, in reverse order, until the email is received by the recipient's email client.

In this chapter, we've explored the **OSI model** and its seven layers, each responsible for a specific part of data communication. Understanding these layers helps network professionals troubleshoot issues, understand how data travels, and design more efficient networks. The real-world example of sending an email illustrates how data flows through each layer, from the application on your computer to the recipient's inbox.

CHAPTER 9

TCP/IP MODEL AND PROTOCOLS

Difference Between OSI and TCP/IP

Both the **OSI model** and the **TCP/IP model** are frameworks used to understand how data moves across a network, but they differ in their structure and approach.

1. **OSI Model** (Open Systems Interconnection):
   - **7 Layers**: The OSI model consists of seven layers: Physical, Data Link, Network, Transport, Session, Presentation, and Application.
   - **Purpose**: It provides a comprehensive framework for understanding network communication and is more focused on the theoretical aspects of networking.
   - **Function**: The OSI model is highly detailed and aims to separate different network functions into discrete layers, making it easier to troubleshoot and design networks.
2. **TCP/IP Model** (Transmission Control Protocol/Internet Protocol):
   - **4 Layers**: The TCP/IP model consists of four layers: Link, Internet, Transport, and Application.

- Purpose: It is the practical framework used for the internet and most modern networks, particularly focusing on the protocols that support networking.
- Function: The TCP/IP model is more focused on real-world functionality and has been widely adopted for internet and network communication. Unlike OSI, the TCP/IP model combines some of the layers (like the OSI Session, Presentation, and Application layers) into a single Application layer.

Key Protocols: TCP, UDP, IP

In the TCP/IP model, **key protocols** play specific roles at different layers to ensure reliable communication between devices. The three most important protocols in the TCP/IP model are **TCP, UDP**, and **IP**.

1. **TCP (Transmission Control Protocol)** – Transport Layer
   - Purpose: TCP is a **connection-oriented** protocol. It ensures reliable data transmission between two devices by establishing a connection before data is sent, maintaining the integrity of the data, and ensuring that lost or corrupted data is retransmitted.

- o **Key Features**:
  - **Reliable**: Guarantees delivery of data in the correct order.
  - **Flow Control**: Manages the rate of data transfer to prevent congestion.
  - **Error Checking**: Ensures that data is not lost or corrupted during transmission.
- o **Real-World Use**: TCP is used for applications where reliability is essential, such as **web browsing (HTTP/HTTPS), email (SMTP)**, and **file transfers (FTP)**.

2. **UDP (User Datagram Protocol)** – Transport Layer
   - o **Purpose**: UDP is a **connectionless** protocol that sends data without establishing a connection. It is faster than TCP but does not guarantee delivery or the correct order of data.
   - o **Key Features**:
     - **Unreliable**: Does not guarantee delivery, error checking, or data order.
     - **Fast**: Suitable for applications where speed is more important than reliability.
     - **Minimal Overhead**: It has less processing overhead than TCP.
   - o **Real-World Use**: UDP is used for real-time applications like **video streaming**, **voice calls**,

and **online gaming**, where delays (latency) are more problematic than occasional data loss.

3. **IP (Internet Protocol)** – Internet Layer

   o **Purpose**: IP is the **network layer** protocol responsible for addressing and routing data across the internet or local networks. It defines the logical addressing (IP addresses) used to identify devices and ensures that data packets are sent to the correct destination.

   o **Key Features**:

      ▪ **Routing**: IP handles the movement of data across different networks by routing packets.

      ▪ **Addressing**: Every device on the network is assigned a unique **IP address** that identifies it on the internet.

      ▪ **Best-Effort Delivery**: IP doesn't guarantee the delivery of packets, error recovery, or data integrity (this is handled by higher layers like TCP).

   o **Real-World Use**: IP is fundamental for all internet-based communication. Without IP, devices wouldn't know how to find each other on a network.

Real-World Example: How Your Computer Communicates with a
Server

Let's consider the process of your computer **communicating with a server** (for example, when you access a website) and see how the TCP/IP protocols come into play.

1. **Step 1: The Application Layer (TCP/IP)**
   o You open a web browser and type in a URL (e.g., www.example.com).
   o Your browser makes an **HTTP** (HyperText Transfer Protocol) request to the web server. This occurs at the **Application Layer** of the TCP/IP model.
   o **Protocol in Action**: **HTTP** is used to send the request for a webpage from the server.

2. **Step 2: The Transport Layer (TCP/IP)**
   o The browser uses **TCP** to break the HTTP request into smaller data packets, ensuring reliable delivery and error-free transmission.
   o **Protocol in Action**: **TCP** establishes a connection with the server, verifies the packets are in order, and ensures that no data is lost during transmission.

3. **Step 3: The Internet Layer (TCP/IP)**

o The data is passed to the **IP layer**, which assigns an **IP address** to the data packets to ensure they reach the correct destination (the server hosting the website).

o **Protocol in Action**: The **IP** protocol routes the data packets across the internet, directing them from your computer's IP address to the server's IP address.

4. **Step 4: The Link Layer (TCP/IP)**

o The data is then passed down to the **Link Layer**, where the packets are framed and transmitted over the physical medium (like Ethernet cables or Wi-Fi).

o The data is sent over your local network, through your router, and then onto the internet.

5. **Step 5: Server Response**

o Once the request reaches the web server, the server processes the request and sends the webpage data back to your computer.

o The server responds with a series of HTTP responses, again broken down into packets by **TCP**.

o These packets are routed back across the internet by **IP**, transmitted over physical links, and reassembled on your computer.

6. **Step 6: Data Presentation**

o Finally, the browser receives the data and uses **HTTP** to interpret the response, rendering the webpage on your screen.

Throughout this process, the protocols work together:

- **HTTP** (Application Layer) ensures the content request is properly formatted.
- **TCP** (Transport Layer) ensures that the data arrives reliably and in order.
- **IP** (Internet Layer) routes the data across networks and directs it to the right server.
- The **Link Layer** handles the physical transmission over the network.

In this chapter, we've discussed the differences between the **OSI model** and the **TCP/IP model**, highlighting their unique layers. We've also covered key protocols such as **TCP, UDP**, and **IP**, explaining their roles in network communication. Finally, the real-world example of how your computer communicates with a server illustrates how these protocols work together to ensure data is transmitted and received accurately and efficiently across the network.

CHAPTER 10

MAC ADDRESSES AND ARP

What is a MAC Address?

A **MAC address** (Media Access Control address) is a unique identifier assigned to network interfaces for communications on a physical network. It is hardcoded into a device's network interface card (NIC) by the manufacturer and serves as the **hardware address** used to identify devices on a local network.

- **Structure**: A MAC address is typically composed of 6 pairs of hexadecimal digits, separated by colons or dashes. For example, **00:1A:2B:3C:4D:5E**.
    - o The first three pairs represent the **Organizationally Unique Identifier** (OUI), which identifies the manufacturer of the device.
    - o The last three pairs are a unique identifier assigned by the manufacturer to that particular network card.
- **Scope**: The MAC address is used only on the local network (or the **Data Link Layer**, Layer 2 in the OSI model). It is not used for routing data between

different networks; instead, it helps devices identify each other on the same local network.

How the Address Resolution Protocol (ARP) Works

The **Address Resolution Protocol** (ARP) is used to map a known **IP address** to a **MAC address**. While devices use **IP addresses** to communicate across networks, they use **MAC addresses** to communicate locally within a network. Since MAC addresses operate only within a local network, ARP is needed to resolve the MAC address associated with a given IP address.

Here's how ARP works:

1. **ARP Request**:
   o When a device wants to communicate with another device on the same local network and knows its IP address, it sends out an **ARP request**.
   o The ARP request is a broadcast message sent to all devices on the local network. It asks, **"Who has this IP address? Please send me your MAC address."**
   o This broadcast is sent to all devices because the requesting device does not yet know which

device has the corresponding MAC address for the target IP address.

2. **ARP Reply**:
   - o The device that owns the requested IP address responds with an **ARP reply**, sending its MAC address back to the requesting device.
   - o The ARP reply is sent directly to the requesting device (unicast) rather than broadcast to the entire network.

3. **Caching**:
   - o Once the requesting device receives the ARP reply, it stores the IP-to-MAC address mapping in its **ARP cache** for future reference. This way, the device doesn't need to send an ARP request every time it wants to communicate with that IP address.

4. **Expiration**:
   - o The entries in the ARP cache are not permanent. They expire after a certain period (typically a few minutes), after which the device will need to send another ARP request to resolve the MAC address again.

Real-World Example: Connecting a Device to a Network

Let's go through a real-world example of how **ARP** and **MAC addresses** come into play when you connect a device to a network:

1. **Step 1: Device Joins the Network**
   Imagine you just bought a new laptop and connect it to your home Wi-Fi network. The laptop is assigned an **IP address** by your router (via **DHCP**, Dynamic Host Configuration Protocol). Your router knows the laptop's IP address but doesn't know its MAC address yet.

2. **Step 2: ARP Request Sent**
   Now, when your laptop wants to communicate with the router or another device on the local network, it needs to know the MAC address of the router (because it communicates with MAC addresses at the data link layer).
   - Your laptop sends an **ARP request** to the local network, asking, "Who has the IP address 192.168.1.1?" (assuming this is the router's IP).

3. **Step 3: ARP Reply**
   The router receives the ARP request and responds directly to the laptop with its **MAC address**. The

reply says, "I have the IP address 192.168.1.1, and my MAC address is 00:11:22:33:44:55."

4. **Step 4: ARP Cache Storage**
   The laptop stores this MAC-to-IP mapping in its **ARP cache** for future use. So, next time the laptop needs to communicate with the router, it already knows the router's MAC address and doesn't need to send another ARP request.

5. **Step 5: Data Transmission**
   With the MAC address of the router known, the laptop can now send data packets directly to the router. These data packets include the router's **MAC address** in the destination field and the laptop's MAC address in the source field, ensuring they are delivered correctly at the local network level.

6. **Step 6: Communication**
   The router, in turn, uses its own IP address to route data packets to other devices or the internet. It may use ARP to find the MAC address of the destination device on a different network (if it's communicating with a device outside the local network) or within the same network.

In this chapter, we've explored the concept of **MAC addresses** and the function of **ARP** (Address Resolution Protocol) in resolving the IP address to MAC address mappings. ARP plays a critical role in enabling communication within a local network, ensuring that devices can find each other and exchange data using both their IP and MAC addresses. The real-world example of connecting a laptop to a network demonstrates how ARP ensures smooth communication and data transfer between devices in a local network.

CHAPTER 11

HOW DATA TRAVELS ON A NETWORK

Packet-Switching and Circuit-Switching

When data is transmitted over a network, it can be sent using either **packet-switching** or **circuit-switching**. These are two different methods of transmitting data that vary in how the network allocates resources and handles communication.

1. **Packet-Switching**:
    - **What it is**: In packet-switching, data is broken down into small, manageable units called **packets**. Each packet contains a piece of the data, as well as the destination address and other control information.
    - **How it works**: These packets are sent across the network independently, taking different paths to reach their destination. Once all the packets arrive at the destination, they are reassembled in the correct order to form the original data.
    - **Advantages**:
        - Efficient use of network resources since multiple packets can take different routes based on network conditions.

81

- Better for handling large amounts of data and internet traffic, as it doesn't require dedicated connections for each communication.
- o **Real-world use**: The internet primarily uses packet-switching to deliver emails, web pages, and streaming data. For example, when you load a webpage, your browser requests the content, which is sent in packets.

2. **Circuit-Switching**:
   - o **What it is**: In circuit-switching, a dedicated communication path or **circuit** is established between the sender and the receiver for the entire duration of the communication session.
   - o **How it works**: The circuit is reserved exclusively for the data transfer, ensuring a constant, predictable data stream. Once the communication is completed, the circuit is terminated.
   - o **Advantages**:
     - Provides a continuous, stable connection with minimal delay.
     - Ideal for real-time communication like voice calls, where uninterrupted transmission is required.
   - o **Real-world use**: Traditional **telephone networks** and **landline calls** rely on circuit-

switching to maintain a constant connection between callers.

Data Transmission Basics: Bits, Bytes, and Frames

Understanding how data is transmitted on a network requires knowledge of the basic units of data—**bits**, **bytes**, and **frames**.

1. **Bits**:
   - A **bit** (short for **binary digit**) is the smallest unit of data in computing, represented by either a **0** or a **1**.
   - In networking, bits are the raw signals transmitted over the network medium (such as electrical pulses, radio waves, or light signals).

2. **Bytes**:
   - A **byte** consists of 8 bits and is the next logical unit of data in networking. A byte is often used to represent a single character (e.g., a letter, number, or symbol).
   - For example, the letter **A** in the ASCII encoding is represented by the byte **01000001** (which equals 65 in decimal).

3. **Frames**:
   - A **frame** is a data packet at the **Data Link Layer** (Layer 2 of the OSI model) and contains not only

the data but also the **MAC addresses** (source and destination), error-checking information, and other control information necessary for data transmission within a local network.

o   Frames are used in technologies like **Ethernet** and **Wi-Fi**. They ensure that data is sent in manageable, structured chunks that can be understood by both the sender and the receiver.

In summary:

- **Bits** are the basic building blocks of data transmission.
- **Bytes** group bits together to represent meaningful information.
- **Frames** are how data is organized and transmitted across local networks.

Real-World Example: Sending and Receiving Data Over Wi-Fi

Let's go through the process of sending and receiving data over Wi-Fi (a wireless network) as a real-world example of how data travels across a network using packet-switching and frames.

1. **Step 1: Requesting Data**
   o   Imagine you're using your smartphone to visit a website. You open the browser and type the URL.

The browser sends a request to the Wi-Fi router for the data (the webpage) from the web server.

o **Packet-Switching**: The request is split into smaller data packets by the smartphone and transmitted over the Wi-Fi network to the router, which then forwards them to the appropriate server.

2. **Step 2: Data Transmission**

o Each data packet that is sent from your smartphone to the router contains not only the data but also control information, such as the source and destination IP addresses, and a checksum to verify data integrity.

o The packets may take different routes through the network, depending on congestion, network conditions, and the available paths.

o **Bits and Bytes**: These packets contain the data for the webpage, which is initially in bits and bytes, representing text, images, and other media.

3. **Step 3: Router and Server**

o The router receives the packets and forwards them to the web server, which processes the request and sends the requested data back to the router in the form of additional packets.

o The web server breaks the webpage data into smaller packets (using packet-switching) and sends them back over the internet to your router, which passes them to your smartphone via the Wi-Fi connection.

4. **Step 4: Reassembling the Data**

   o The smartphone receives the incoming packets and reassembles them into the original webpage using the control information (such as sequence numbers) contained in each packet.

   o The smartphone processes the packets, assembling the text, images, and other content into a readable webpage.

5. **Step 5: Error Checking and Acknowledgment**

   o Along the way, **TCP** (Transport Layer Protocol) ensures that the data is received correctly by performing error checking. If any packets are lost or corrupted, the smartphone will request retransmission of those specific packets.

   o The router and web server also handle the **frame** level, ensuring that the data is properly framed with MAC addresses for local network communication.

6. **Step 6: Displaying the Webpage**

   o Once all packets are received and reassembled, the webpage is displayed on your smartphone. You can now browse and interact with the website, sending and receiving more data as needed.

Throughout this process, the data is divided into smaller units, transmitted efficiently over the network, and reassembled to deliver the full content to your device. The use of **packet-switching**, **bits**, **bytes**, and **frames** ensures that the data can travel efficiently and securely across the network.

In this chapter, we've discussed how data travels across a network using **packet-switching** and **circuit-switching**, and we've explained the basic units of data transmission, including **bits**, **bytes**, and **frames**. Through the real-world example of sending and receiving data over Wi-Fi, we've shown how these concepts come together to enable efficient communication in modern networks. Whether you're browsing the web, streaming video, or sending emails, packet-switching and data frames are at the heart of network communication.

CHAPTER 12

ROUTING AND SWITCHING

How Routers and Switches Manage Data

Both **routers** and **switches** are essential networking devices that manage the flow of data across a network. However, they serve different roles in terms of how data is transmitted and handled, and they operate at different layers of the OSI model.

1. **Routers**:
   - o **Function**: A router is responsible for directing data packets between different networks. It connects multiple networks together and forwards data packets to their destination based on their **IP address**.
   - o **Layer**: Routers operate at the **Network Layer** (Layer 3) of the OSI model. They use the **IP address** in the packet header to determine the best path for the data to travel to reach its destination, often through the use of **routing tables**.
   - o **How It Works**: When a device sends data to a destination outside its local network, the data is forwarded to a router. The router examines the

destination IP address and checks its routing table to find the most efficient path to the destination. The router then forwards the data packet to the next router or destination.

2. **Switches**:

   o **Function**: A switch is used to connect devices within a local network (such as a home or office network) and forwards data packets to the correct device based on the **MAC address**.

   o **Layer**: Switches operate at the **Data Link Layer** (Layer 2) of the OSI model. They use **MAC addresses** to determine where to send data within the same local network.

   o **How It Works**: When a device sends data, the switch reads the destination MAC address and forwards the data only to the device with the matching MAC address. This allows for more efficient communication within the local network, as it reduces unnecessary traffic to other devices.

Key Differences Between Routers and Switches:

- **Routers** connect different networks and use **IP addresses** to determine where to forward data.

- **Switches** connect devices within the same network and use **MAC addresses** to forward data efficiently.

Real-World Example: A Message Passing Through Different Networks

Let's explore how data flows through multiple routers and switches when sending a message from one device to another, especially when that message has to travel across different networks (such as from your home network to a server on the internet).

1. **Step 1: Sending the Message from Your Computer**

   o You send an email or request a webpage on your computer (using a **web browser** or email client). The computer generates data packets that contain the message, with the **destination IP address** of the web server or email recipient.

   o At this point, the data is in the form of **packets** with destination and source IP addresses.

2. **Step 2: Local Network (Switching)**

   o The data is first sent to the **switch** within your home or office network. The switch reads the **MAC address** of the destination device (for example, a printer, another computer, or a router).

   o If the destination is not within the local network, the switch forwards the data to the router (which is the gateway to other networks). If the destination is a device within the same local network, the switch will send it directly to that device based on the MAC address.

3. **Step 3: Router Determines the Path (Routing)**

   o   If the destination is outside the local network (such as a website or a remote server), the data is forwarded to the **router**. The router examines the **destination IP address** in the packet header.

   o   The router uses its **routing table** to determine the best path to the destination. It may forward the packet to another router or directly to the destination server, depending on the network configuration and the path available.

4. **Step 4: Data Travels Across the Internet**

   o   The router sends the packet to another router, which continues the journey. As the packet travels through the internet, it may pass through several different routers, each checking the destination IP address and forwarding the packet along the most efficient route.

   o   The routers may use **different routing protocols** (e.g., **BGP** or **OSPF**) to exchange information and determine the best path.

5. **Step 5: Arriving at the Destination Network**

- o Once the data packet reaches the destination network (for example, a website's server), it is forwarded to the correct device (the web server) by the switch within the destination network.
- o The server processes the request (for example, loading the requested webpage or delivering an email), and the response is sent back to the originating device (your computer) following the same process.

6. **Step 6: Return Journey**
   - o The process is reversed when the response (such as a webpage or email data) is sent back to your computer. The web server or email server sends data packets back to the destination IP (your computer's IP address), traveling through multiple routers, switches, and networks.
   - o Each router along the way checks the destination IP address and forwards the data until it arrives at your local network, where the data is delivered by the switch to your computer.

In this chapter, we've explained how **routers** and **switches** manage data within a network. Routers direct traffic between different networks, while switches forward data within a local network. The real-world example of how a message (data) passes through different networks shows how data is routed across the internet, traveling through multiple devices and networks before reaching its destination. This process relies on both **routing** (via IP addresses) and **switching** (via MAC addresses) to ensure efficient and reliable communication.

CHAPTER 13

DNS AND DOMAIN NAME SYSTEM

What is DNS?

DNS (Domain Name System) is essentially the "phonebook" of the internet. It is a system used to translate human-readable domain names, such as www.example.com, into machine-readable **IP addresses** (such as **192.168.1.1**). Every device on the internet, including websites, servers, and your computer, is identified by an IP address. However, IP addresses are not easy for humans to remember, which is why DNS is so crucial—without it, we would have to type in long strings of numbers to visit websites.

DNS is a hierarchical system consisting of multiple servers that work together to resolve domain names into IP addresses. It ensures that users can access websites and online services by typing in a simple and familiar domain name instead of dealing with complex numerical IP addresses.

How Domain Names Are Resolved into IP Addresses

When you type a domain name into your web browser, the browser needs to find out the corresponding IP address of the server that hosts the website. Here's how the process works:

1. **Step 1: Browser Sends DNS Query**
   o When you enter a URL (e.g., www.example.com) into your browser, the browser first checks if the corresponding **IP address** is already stored in its **cache** (the browser may have recently accessed the website, so it might already know the IP).
   o If the IP address is not cached, the browser sends a request (called a **DNS query**) to the operating system's DNS resolver.

2. **Step 2: Resolver Checks Local Cache**
   o The operating system's **DNS resolver** checks its own cache to see if it has recently looked up the IP address for the domain. If the IP address is in the cache, it sends it back to the browser, allowing the website to load quickly.
   o If the IP address isn't cached, the resolver forwards the query to a **recursive DNS server**.

3. **Step 3: Recursive DNS Server Queries**

o The **recursive DNS server** is responsible for resolving the domain name. If the recursive server doesn't know the IP address, it queries other DNS servers starting from the **root DNS servers**.

4. **Step 4: Root DNS Servers**

o Root DNS servers are the highest-level servers in the DNS hierarchy. There are 13 sets of these servers, distributed across the globe. They don't store domain information directly but rather direct the query to more specific servers that do.

o The recursive DNS server sends the query to a **Top-Level Domain (TLD) DNS server**, such as the one that handles **.com**, **.org**, or **.net** domain extensions.

5. **Step 5: TLD DNS Servers**

o The TLD DNS server takes the query for www.example.com and returns the IP address of the **Authoritative DNS Server** for **example.com**.

6. **Step 6: Authoritative DNS Servers**

o The **Authoritative DNS server** contains the actual IP address for www.example.com (or other subdomains). It responds to the recursive server with the correct IP address for the requested domain.

7. **Step 7: IP Address Sent Back**
   - The recursive DNS server sends the IP address back to the operating system's resolver, which in turn sends it to the browser.
   - The browser can now use the IP address to connect to the website's server and retrieve the webpage content.

8. **Step 8: Website Loads**
   - The website loads, and the browser caches the IP address for future use, improving speed the next time you visit that domain.

This entire process typically takes milliseconds, which is why we don't notice it happening.

Real-World Example: Visiting a Website by Domain Name

Let's walk through a real-world example to see how DNS resolves domain names into IP addresses when you visit a website.

1. **Step 1: Entering the Domain Name**
   - You open your web browser and type www.example.com into the address bar.

2. **Step 2: DNS Query**
   - Your browser checks its cache to see if it has the IP address for www.example.com. If it doesn't, it

asks the operating system's DNS resolver to find it.

3. **Step 3: Operating System and Recursive DNS Query**

   o The operating system's DNS resolver sends the DNS query to a **recursive DNS server** (usually provided by your ISP or a third-party DNS service like Google DNS or OpenDNS).

4. **Step 4: Recursive DNS Server Starts the Resolution Process**

   o The recursive DNS server doesn't have the IP address either, so it asks a **root DNS server** for the IP address of www.example.com.

   o The root DNS server replies with the address of the **TLD DNS server** for **.com**.

5. **Step 5: TLD DNS Server**

   o The recursive DNS server queries the **.com TLD DNS server**, which replies with the IP address of the **Authoritative DNS server** for **example.com**.

6. **Step 6: Authoritative DNS Server**

   o The recursive DNS server now sends a query to the **Authoritative DNS server** for **example.com**, which responds with the IP address for www.example.com (let's say it's **93.184.216.34**).

7. **Step 7: Returning the IP Address**

- The recursive DNS server sends the IP address (**93.184.216.34**) back to the operating system's DNS resolver, which passes it on to the browser.

8. **Step 8: Connecting to the Website**

   - Now that the browser has the IP address for www.example.com, it can establish a connection to the server at **93.184.216.34** and request the webpage content.
   - The webpage is returned to your browser, and you can see the website.

Throughout this process, the DNS system allows you to access websites by typing in friendly, human-readable domain names rather than long, complicated IP addresses.

In this chapter, we've explored the **DNS** system and how it resolves domain names into IP addresses. From checking local caches to querying root DNS servers and authoritative servers, DNS ensures that users can seamlessly navigate the internet without needing to memorize numeric IP addresses. The real-world example of visiting www.example.com demonstrates how DNS works behind the scenes to make the web user-friendly and accessible.

CHAPTER 14

THE ROLE OF FIREWALLS AND SECURITY IN NETWORKING

What Are Firewalls and How Do They Protect Networks?

A **firewall** is a security device or software that monitors and controls incoming and outgoing network traffic based on predetermined security rules. Its primary role is to act as a barrier or filter between a trusted internal network (like your home or office network) and untrusted external networks (like the internet). Firewalls can be hardware-based, software-based, or a combination of both.

Firewalls protect networks in several ways:

1. **Traffic Filtering**:
    o Firewalls examine the data packets being transmitted across a network and decide whether they should be allowed through based on predefined rules. These rules might specify allowed IP addresses, specific types of traffic (such as HTTP or FTP), and permitted ports.
    o **Allow or Block**: If a packet matches a rule (for example, an approved IP address or application),

100

the firewall allows it to pass. If it doesn't match, the packet is blocked.

2. **Inbound and Outbound Traffic Control**:

   o   Firewalls monitor both **incoming** and **outgoing** traffic. For example, if an external attacker tries to access a device on the internal network, the firewall can block the attacker's IP address. Similarly, if internal devices are attempting to access unauthorized websites or send sensitive data, the firewall can block these actions as well.

3. **Packet Inspection**:

   o   Firewalls use various techniques to inspect data packets. Some firewalls simply look at the header information (such as the source and destination IP addresses), while others can perform **deep packet inspection**, analyzing the entire packet to detect malicious content.

4. **Preventing Unauthorized Access**:

   o   Firewalls protect networks from unauthorized access by ensuring that only legitimate traffic (from trusted sources or applications) can reach the network. This is especially important for preventing cyberattacks, such as **denial-of-service attacks (DoS)**, **malware**, or **hacking attempts**.

5. **Virtual Private Network (VPN) Support**:

- o Many firewalls support the use of **VPNs** (Virtual Private Networks), which allow secure communication between remote devices and the local network by encrypting the traffic. VPNs help keep the data private and secure even over unsecured networks like the internet.

6. **NAT (Network Address Translation)**:
   - o Firewalls often implement **NAT** to hide the internal IP addresses of devices within a network. This provides an additional layer of security by preventing external entities from directly accessing internal devices.

Types of Firewalls

There are different types of firewalls, each with specific features:

1. **Packet-Filtering Firewalls**:
   - o The most basic type of firewall. It inspects packets at the **Network Layer** (Layer 3) and checks the source, destination, and port number. If the packet matches an allowed rule, it's forwarded; otherwise, it's dropped.

2. **Stateful Inspection Firewalls**:
   - o These firewalls track the state of active connections and make decisions based on the

context of the traffic. They inspect packets more thoroughly than packet-filtering firewalls, considering whether the traffic is part of an established connection.

3. **Proxy Firewalls**:

   o   Proxy firewalls act as intermediaries between users and the services they are accessing. They can hide the internal network, making it harder for attackers to pinpoint or access specific devices.

4. **Next-Generation Firewalls (NGFW)**:

   o   NGFWs go beyond traditional firewalls by including features like **deep packet inspection, intrusion detection, application awareness,** and **cloud-delivered threat intelligence**. These firewalls are capable of defending against more sophisticated and evolving threats.

Real-World Example: Home Firewall Setup for Safety

Let's take a look at a real-world example of setting up a **home firewall** to protect your home network.

1. **Step   1:   Choosing   a   Firewall** In a typical home setup, you'll have a router that often comes with a built-in firewall. Many modern

routers also have the capability to perform basic packet filtering, stateful inspection, and NAT. If you want additional protection, you can install a software firewall on individual devices or use a dedicated hardware firewall (such as a firewall appliance) in your home network.

2. **Step 2: Configuring the Router's Firewall Settings**

   o **Default Configuration**: Most routers come with a default firewall setting that blocks unsolicited incoming traffic from the internet while allowing outgoing traffic from devices in your home. This setup protects your devices from external threats like hackers.

   o **Port Forwarding**: If you need to access a device in your home network (e.g., a security camera or a gaming console) from the outside world, you'll need to configure **port forwarding** on your router. However, this should be done carefully, as it opens specific ports on your network to the internet. A well-configured firewall will only allow authorized traffic on specific ports.

   o **Block Unnecessary Services**: Disable services like **UPnP** (Universal Plug and Play) if they are not needed, as they can expose your network to security risks.

3. **Step 3: Creating Rules for Access Control**

   o Many home firewalls allow you to configure rules based on IP addresses, application types, or ports. For example, you can block access to certain websites or services during specific hours (e.g., restricting internet access for kids during homework time).

   o **Blocking Unwanted Traffic**: You can create rules to block traffic from suspicious IP addresses, or prevent devices in your home network from connecting to certain external services (such as social media or file-sharing sites).

4. **Step 4: Enabling Intrusion Detection/Prevention**

   o Some home routers offer additional security features like **Intrusion Detection Systems (IDS)** or **Intrusion Prevention Systems (IPS)**, which monitor for unusual or malicious activity. These systems can block potential threats like malware or unauthorized access attempts before they can harm your network.

5. **Step 5: Setting Up a VPN**

   o For additional security, you can configure a **VPN** on your home router, which encrypts all the traffic between your devices and the internet. This is particularly useful when using public Wi-

Fi networks, as it ensures your personal data is protected from eavesdropping.

6. **Step 6: Regular Updates**

   o It's important to regularly update your router's firmware and software firewall to ensure that you have the latest security patches and protections against new threats. Firewalls need to be continuously updated to handle emerging threats such as **zero-day vulnerabilities**.

In this chapter, we've explored how **firewalls** protect networks by controlling and filtering traffic, preventing unauthorized access, and providing security from cyber threats. We also reviewed the different types of firewalls and their functions. The **home firewall setup example** illustrated how to configure a router's built-in firewall to protect your home network and devices. With a well-configured firewall in place, your network is better protected against external attacks, providing a safer online environment for your devices.

CHAPTER 15

UNDERSTANDING PORTS AND PROTOCOLS

What Are Ports and Why Do They Matter?

Ports are numerical identifiers used by operating systems and network devices to manage multiple communication channels over a single network connection. When data is sent over the internet, it is not just directed to a specific device (via its IP address), but also to a specific **port** on that device. Each port serves a particular purpose and corresponds to a specific service or application running on the device.

Ports act as entry and exit points for data. When a device sends data to another device, it specifies both the **IP address** (to identify the device) and the **port number** (to identify the service or application on the device).

- **Why they matter**: Ports help direct the data to the right application. For example, when you request a webpage, the data is sent to **port 80** on the server, which is the default port for **HTTP** traffic. If the data were sent to a different port, the server wouldn't recognize the request for the webpage and would reject the connection.

There are two categories of ports:

1. **Well-known Ports**: These are reserved for specific services and protocols. They are numbered from **0 to 1023**.

2. **Ephemeral or Dynamic Ports**: These are temporary ports assigned by the operating system for short-term connections. They range from **1024 to 65535** and are typically used for client-side applications.

Common Ports for Popular Protocols (HTTP, FTP, etc.)

Several well-known protocols are associated with specific ports. Below are some common ports and the protocols they are used with:

1. **HTTP (HyperText Transfer Protocol)**
   o **Port 80**: HTTP is the protocol used for transferring webpages. When you access a website without encryption (i.e., **http://**), the communication takes place over **port 80**.

2. **HTTPS (HyperText Transfer Protocol Secure)**
   o **Port 443**: HTTPS is the secure version of HTTP, using encryption (SSL/TLS). It is used for transferring webpages securely (i.e., **https://**). Data is encrypted to protect privacy and security.

3. **FTP (File Transfer Protocol)**

- o **Port 21**: FTP is a protocol used to transfer files between systems on a network. Port 21 is the control port used for sending commands to the FTP server.
- o **Port 20**: Used for transferring data during an active FTP session.

4. SMTP (Simple Mail Transfer Protocol)

- o **Port 25**: SMTP is used for sending emails between mail servers. When you send an email from your email client (like Outlook or Gmail), it uses **port 25** to communicate with the email server.

5. IMAP (Internet Message Access Protocol)

- o **Port 143**: IMAP is used by email clients to retrieve messages from a mail server. It allows users to organize, delete, and search their email messages on the server.

6. POP3 (Post Office Protocol 3)

- o **Port 110**: POP3 is another protocol used for retrieving email from a server. Unlike IMAP, POP3 typically downloads the messages to the client and deletes them from the server.

7. SSH (Secure Shell)

- o **Port 22**: SSH is a secure protocol used to remotely log into a server and execute commands. It provides encrypted communication to protect sensitive data from eavesdropping.

8. **DNS (Domain Name System)**

   o **Port 53**: DNS is used to translate domain names (like www.example.com) into IP addresses. When you type a URL into a web browser, your computer uses DNS over **port 53** to resolve the domain name to an IP address.

Real-World Example: Accessing a Website (Port 80)

Let's walk through how **port 80** plays a role in accessing a website:

1. **Step 1: Requesting the Website**

   o You open your browser and type www.example.com into the address bar.

   o The browser creates a **HTTP request** to the website. This request is directed to **port 80** on the server that hosts www.example.com.

2. **Step 2: DNS Resolution**

   o Before the request reaches the website's server, your browser first needs to resolve www.example.com into an IP address.

   o It sends a **DNS query** (on **port 53**) to a DNS server to find the IP address of www.example.com.

110

o The DNS server responds with the IP address of the server hosting the website.

3. **Step 3: Sending Data to Port 80**

   o Now that the browser has the IP address of the website's server, it sends the **HTTP request** to **port 80** on the server.

   o The request contains information such as the type of browser, the specific page requested, and other headers.

   o The server receives the request on **port 80** and processes it.

4. **Step 4: Server Response**

   o The server sends the requested webpage back to your browser as a series of **HTTP responses**.

   o The webpage data is sent to your browser in small packets, and the browser reconstructs the webpage.

5. **Step 5: Displaying the Webpage**

   o Your browser displays the webpage, now that it has received and assembled the data. You can now interact with the site by clicking links, entering text, and more.

6. **Step 6: Closing the Connection**

   o Once the data is delivered, the connection to **port 80** is closed, and the communication session ends.

111

In this process, **port 80** is used for the HTTP protocol to communicate between your browser and the server hosting the website. The request and response are both transmitted through this port, making it the default channel for web traffic.

In this chapter, we've discussed the importance of **ports** in managing network traffic, helping direct data to the correct application or service. We also explored common ports associated with popular protocols such as **HTTP, FTP**, and **SMTP**. The real-world example of accessing a website demonstrated how **port 80** plays a key role in the communication process, allowing your browser to request and receive data from a web server. Understanding ports and protocols is essential for network management, troubleshooting, and security.

Part 4

Types of Networks and Connectivity

CHAPTER 16

LAN, WAN, AND MAN: UNDERSTANDING NETWORK TYPES

Differences Between Local Area Networks (LAN), Wide Area Networks (WAN), and Metropolitan Area Networks (MAN)

Networking is categorized into different types based on the geographic area they cover, the number of devices they support, and their complexity. The three most common types of networks are **Local Area Networks (LAN), Wide Area Networks (WAN)**, and **Metropolitan Area Networks (MAN)**. Let's explore each of these networks and understand their differences:

1. **Local Area Network (LAN):**
   o **Definition**: A **LAN** is a network that covers a small geographical area, typically within a building or campus, such as a home, office, or school. LANs are designed to connect a relatively small number of devices (e.g., computers, printers, smartphones, etc.) and enable them to share resources like files, printers, and internet access.

- o **Characteristics**:
  - **Small Area**: Covers a limited geographic area like a single building or floor.
  - **High-Speed**: LANs usually offer high-speed connections, typically through **Ethernet cables** or **Wi-Fi**.
  - **Private Ownership**: Typically owned, managed, and maintained by a single organization or individual.
  - **Examples**: A home network connecting your laptop, smartphone, and smart TV; a corporate office network connecting computers and printers.

2. **Wide Area Network (WAN)**:
   - o **Definition**: A **WAN** spans a large geographical area, often covering cities, countries, or even continents. WANs are used to connect multiple LANs and allow communication across long distances, typically via leased lines, fiber-optic cables, or satellite links.
   - o **Characteristics**:
     - **Large Area**: Covers vast geographical distances, connecting multiple cities or even countries.
     - **Lower Speed**: WAN connections are generally slower than LAN connections

115

due to the long distances involved and the complexity of the infrastructure.

- **Public/Private Ownership**: WANs may be owned by multiple organizations or service providers, and in some cases, they are public, like the **Internet**.

- **Examples**: The **Internet** itself is the largest WAN, connecting millions of LANs globally; connecting multiple branch offices of a company in different cities or countries via VPN.

3. **Metropolitan Area Network (MAN)**:

   o **Definition**: A **MAN** is a network that covers a larger area than a LAN but is smaller than a WAN. Typically, a MAN covers a **city** or a large campus and is often used to connect multiple LANs within that area. MANs can be used to provide high-speed internet or private data services to businesses or organizations in that region.

   o **Characteristics**:

      - **Moderate Area**: Covers a city or metropolitan area, connecting different LANs within that city.

116

- **High-Speed Connections**: Generally offers higher speeds than WANs, but lower than LANs.

- **Public/Private Ownership**: Can be owned by a service provider or government and used for public or private purposes.

- **Examples**: City-wide Wi-Fi networks, public transportation systems' communication networks, or large universities with multiple campuses across a city connected via a MAN.

Real-World Example: Connecting Multiple Offices in a City Versus a Single Home Network

Let's look at two practical examples to understand how LAN, WAN, and MAN work in different settings:

1. **Single Home Network (LAN)**:
   - Imagine you have a **home network** in your house, which connects your laptop, smartphone, tablet, and printer. This is a **LAN** because it operates within a **small area** (your home) and connects a limited number of devices.

117

o   All devices in this home network can share resources like the internet, printers, and files. The router serves as the central device, allowing these devices to communicate with each other and access the internet. The network is private and typically managed by you, the homeowner.

o   **Connection Type**: The devices in the home network are either connected by **Wi-Fi** or **Ethernet cables**, providing fast and reliable communication within the house.

2. **Multiple Offices in a City (MAN/WAN)**:

o   Imagine you are working for a company with **multiple offices** in a **city**. Each office has its own **LAN**, but the company needs to connect them to enable communication between employees, access to shared files, and centralized services. This is where a **MAN** or **WAN** comes in.

o   **MAN Example**: If the company has offices in multiple locations within the same city (e.g., three offices in New York City), they could set up a **MAN** to connect all the offices. The MAN would ensure that each office can share resources like internal servers, databases, and applications quickly, without relying on the public internet.

- The MAN might be set up using high-speed fiber-optic cables or leased lines that run between the different office buildings. It would offer relatively high-speed communication between the offices, enabling them to share large files, conduct video conferences, and collaborate in real-time.

○ **WAN Example**: If the company has offices in different cities or countries (e.g., New York, London, and Tokyo), the company would need to set up a **WAN**. This could involve connecting the different office LANs through a **VPN** (Virtual Private Network) or using private leased lines or satellite links. The WAN would allow employees in all offices to access the same resources and communicate with each other, even though they are located across long distances.

- The WAN would provide secure communication between offices, but it may be slower than the MAN due to the

119

greater distances involved and the complexity of the infrastructure.

Key Differences Recap:

- **LAN**: Small area, high speed, private ownership (e.g., home network).
- **WAN**: Large area, lower speed, can be public/private, connects multiple LANs (e.g., Internet, connecting global offices).
- **MAN**: Moderate area (city), high speed, private/public, connects multiple LANs within a city (e.g., city-wide network for businesses).

In this chapter, we've explored the differences between **LANs**, **WANs**, and **MANs** and how each type of network serves different purposes based on the geographical area, speed, and number of devices involved. The **real-world examples** of a single home network (LAN) and connecting multiple offices in a city (MAN) versus across cities (WAN) help to demonstrate how these network types work in practice. Each network type plays a crucial role in how we communicate and share resources in different settings.

CHAPTER 17

WIRELESS NETWORKING: WI-FI AND BEYOND

How Wireless Networks Work

Wireless networks use **radio waves** to transmit data between devices, allowing them to communicate without the need for physical cables. These networks operate by sending and receiving data through airwaves, which are part of the electromagnetic spectrum, much like the way radio or TV signals are transmitted. The most common wireless network technology in use today is **Wi-Fi**, but other wireless technologies such as **Bluetooth**, **Zigbee**, and **5G** are also widely used for specific applications.

Here's a basic breakdown of how **Wi-Fi** (the most common wireless networking technology) works:

1. **Access Point (AP):**
   At the core of any wireless network is the **access point** (AP), which is typically a **Wi-Fi router**. The access point is a device that connects to the internet or an internal network using a wired connection (usually Ethernet) and then transmits data over radio

waves to **wireless devices** like smartphones, laptops, tablets, and smart TVs.

2. **Radio Frequency (RF) Communication**: Wi-Fi works by transmitting data through radio frequencies (RF), which are electromagnetic waves that travel through the air. These frequencies are divided into channels that devices use to send and receive data. Common Wi-Fi frequencies are **2.4 GHz** and **5 GHz** bands, with newer technologies like **Wi-Fi 6** supporting higher frequencies like **6 GHz**.

3. **Modulation and Demodulation**: When data is sent over Wi-Fi, it is first encoded into a format suitable for transmission over radio waves. This is called **modulation**. The access point modulates the data into radio waves, and the wireless devices **demodulate** the waves to retrieve the data. The reverse happens when the devices send data back to the router.

4. **Wireless Standards**: The **IEEE 802.11** family of standards defines how Wi-Fi networks operate. These standards evolve over time to offer faster speeds, better range, and increased reliability. The most common Wi-Fi standards are:

- o **802.11b/g/n** (older standards with lower speeds)
- o **802.11ac** (Wi-Fi 5, providing faster speeds and better performance)
- o **802.11ax** (Wi-Fi 6, the latest standard offering faster speeds and more efficient use of spectrum)

5. **Security**:

Wireless networks are vulnerable to interception and unauthorized access. To protect data, Wi-Fi networks are secured using **encryption** protocols such as **WPA2** (Wi-Fi Protected Access) and **WPA3**, which prevent unauthorized users from accessing the network and protect the data being transmitted.

Real-World Example: Setting Up a Home Wi-Fi Network

Let's walk through the process of setting up a **home Wi-Fi network** and understand how the wireless technology comes into play:

1. **Step 1: Choose a Wi-Fi Router/Access Point**
   - o The first step in setting up a home Wi-Fi network is purchasing a **Wi-Fi router** (which often functions as an access point). You can choose between routers that support different Wi-Fi standards (e.g., **Wi-Fi 5** or **Wi-Fi 6**). A router

with **Wi-Fi 6** will provide faster speeds and better performance for more devices, but a **Wi-Fi 5** router is typically sufficient for most households.

o   Some routers also include additional features like **dual-band** support, which means they can operate on both **2.4 GHz** and **5 GHz** frequencies, allowing for better flexibility and performance.

2. **Step 2: Connect the Router to the Internet**

o   The router needs to be connected to the internet. If you have a **fiber-optic, DSL**, or **cable** internet connection, the router will be connected to the **modem** provided by your ISP (Internet Service Provider). The modem converts the internet signal into a form that the router can understand and broadcast over Wi-Fi.

o   Plug the **Ethernet cable** from the modem into the **WAN (Wide Area Network) port** on the router.

3. **Step 3: Configure the Wi-Fi Router**

o   Once the router is physically connected, you'll need to access the router's **web interface** (usually via a browser on a computer or smartphone) to set up your Wi-Fi network.

o   You'll be prompted to configure settings such as the **SSID** (Service Set Identifier, which is the name of your Wi-Fi network), **password**, and **security protocol**. Most routers default to **WPA2** or **WPA3**, which are secure methods of encryption for the network.

4. **Step 4: Set the Wireless Channels**

   o   In the router's settings, you can configure the wireless **channel** used by your Wi-Fi network. Wi-Fi channels are like lanes on a highway. If you're in a crowded area (e.g., an apartment complex), selecting a less crowded channel can help reduce interference. Many routers automatically choose the best channel, but you can manually select one if needed.

5. **Step 5: Connecting Devices to the Network**

   o   After setting up the router, you can now connect your wireless devices. Simply go to the **Wi-Fi settings** on each device (laptop, smartphone, tablet, etc.), select the **SSID** you created for your network, and enter the password.

   o   Once connected, each device can send and receive data wirelessly through the router, allowing you to browse the web, stream videos, and access shared files.

6. **Step 6: Ensuring Security and Optimization**

   o   **Change Default Passwords**: If you haven't already, make sure to change any default admin passwords on your router to avoid unauthorized access to the router's settings.

- o **Enable WPA3 Encryption**: If your router supports **WPA3**, it's advisable to enable it for the latest and most secure encryption.
- o **Limit Device Access**: You can set up **guest networks** for visitors, ensuring they don't have access to your main network and its shared resources.

7. **Step 7: Enjoy Your Wireless Network**
   - o After completing the setup, your home network is now ready to be used. You can access the internet, share files between devices, print wirelessly, stream media, and enjoy a smooth, wireless internet experience.

In this chapter, we've discussed how **wireless networks** work, with a focus on **Wi-Fi** and the technology behind it, such as radio waves, access points, and encryption. The real-world example of setting up a **home Wi-Fi network** demonstrated the practical steps involved in creating a wireless network in your home, from choosing the right router to connecting devices and ensuring security. Wireless networking makes it easier and more convenient to connect and communicate over the internet without the constraints of physical cables.

CHAPTER 18

CELLULAR NETWORKS: MOBILE CONNECTIVITY

How Cellular Networks Provide Mobile Internet

Cellular networks are the backbone of mobile internet connectivity, enabling communication via mobile phones, tablets, and other devices that rely on cellular data. These networks provide internet access, voice services, and text messaging by using **radio waves** to communicate with cell towers.

Here's a breakdown of how cellular networks work to provide mobile internet:

1. **Cell Towers and Coverage Areas**:
   o The land is divided into smaller areas called **cells**, each of which is covered by a **cell tower**. These cell towers are strategically placed to ensure widespread coverage, and each cell can support multiple users at a time.
   o Each cell tower connects to the **core network**, which is the central hub that provides internet access and routes calls and data to and from the mobile device.

2. **Mobile Device Connection**:

- o When you turn on your mobile device, it searches for nearby cell towers. The device connects to the tower that offers the best signal strength.

- o Once connected to the tower, the device communicates with the **core network** to access the internet or make a call.

- o **Data Transmission**: Data from your device, such as a web page or video, is broken into smaller packets and sent to the cell tower. The cell tower forwards this data to the appropriate network infrastructure (such as internet routers or servers) to retrieve the requested information.

3. **Different Generations of Cellular Networks**:

- o **2G (Second Generation)**: The first digital cellular network, providing basic voice services and limited data speeds for text messaging and very basic internet services.

- o **3G (Third Generation)**: Introduced higher data speeds, allowing for faster mobile internet, video calls, and multimedia streaming.

- o **4G (Fourth Generation)**: Offers high-speed mobile internet with sufficient bandwidth to support high-definition video streaming, online gaming, and video conferencing.

- o **5G (Fifth Generation)**: The latest generation, providing even faster data speeds, lower latency, and more reliable connectivity for advanced applications like autonomous vehicles, smart cities, and augmented reality.

4. **Data Packets and Radio Frequencies**:

- o Just like Wi-Fi, cellular networks use radio waves to transmit data. However, cellular networks use **different radio frequencies** (compared to Wi-Fi) to handle mobile calls, text messages, and internet traffic.

- o The data sent and received by mobile devices is broken into **small packets**, which are sent over the radio waves to the nearest cell tower. The packets are reassembled at the destination, whether that's a website server or another device.

5. **Roaming**:

- o **Roaming** occurs when your mobile device moves out of the coverage area of your home network (e.g., traveling abroad) and connects to another network that supports your mobile carrier. Roaming allows you to continue using mobile data, voice, and text services in regions where your carrier has agreements with local network operators.

Real-World Example: Using Mobile Data in a Remote Area

Let's explore how **mobile data** works in a **remote area** where Wi-Fi access is not available, and the user relies on **cellular data** for internet connectivity.

Imagine you are on a camping trip in a rural area with limited access to Wi-Fi. You need to access maps and search for nearby services. Here's how **mobile data** works in this scenario:

1. **Step 1: Turning on Mobile Data**
   o You turn on **mobile data** on your smartphone. Your phone searches for the nearest **cell tower**. Since you're in a remote area, the coverage may be limited, but you find a nearby tower that provides a weak but sufficient signal.

2. **Step 2: Connecting to the Network**
   o Your device establishes a connection with the cell tower, which is part of the **cellular network**. The tower forwards the connection request to the **core network**, which provides access to the internet and other services.
   o Depending on the generation of the cellular network in the area (e.g., 3G or 4G), the

130

connection may have varying speeds, but it is enough to allow for basic internet use, such as accessing maps or sending messages.

3. **Step 3: Using Mobile Data**

   o   Once connected, you use **mobile data** to access online maps and search for nearby attractions. The data packets from your device are transmitted to the cell tower, which sends them to the core network. The core network then connects you to the internet, retrieves the requested map data, and sends it back to the tower.

   o   The tower transmits the data back to your device, allowing you to view the maps on your phone screen.

4. **Step 4: Roaming (If Applicable)**

   o   If you're in an area where your primary carrier doesn't have coverage but a **partner carrier** does, you might be **roaming**. In this case, the local network forwards your data requests to your home network, and you are billed accordingly (usually at a higher rate for roaming services).

   o   If roaming is enabled, you can still use mobile data, but keep in mind that you may face additional charges depending on your mobile carrier's roaming agreements.

5. **Step 5: Continuing the Journey**

o As you continue your trip, you might move in and out of different cellular coverage areas. If you move out of range of the current cell tower, your phone will automatically connect to another tower to maintain internet connectivity.

o In rural or remote areas, mobile data speeds might slow down as more people use the network, or the cell tower might struggle to provide sufficient bandwidth, leading to slower speeds or intermittent connections.

In this chapter, we've discussed how **cellular networks** provide mobile internet, enabling devices like smartphones and tablets to access the web via **radio waves** through cell towers. We also covered the different generations of cellular networks (2G, 3G, 4G, and 5G) and how they impact internet speed and reliability. The **real-world example** of using **mobile data** in a remote area illustrates how a mobile device connects to a cellular network, communicates with the nearest tower, and accesses the internet. Even in areas without Wi-Fi, mobile data allows users to stay connected on the go.

CHAPTER 19

VPNS: SECURING YOUR CONNECTION

What is a Virtual Private Network (VPN)?

A **Virtual Private Network (VPN)** is a technology that creates a secure, encrypted connection between your device and the internet, routing your internet traffic through a **private server**. VPNs are used to protect your online activities, enhance privacy, and provide secure access to the internet, especially when using public networks like Wi-Fi hotspots.

When you use a VPN, it acts as a **tunnel** for your internet traffic. Your data is encrypted before it leaves your device, preventing third parties, such as hackers or your internet service provider (ISP), from intercepting or monitoring your online activities. The VPN server acts as an intermediary, sending your data to the internet and receiving it back, making it appear as though your connection is coming from the server's location rather than your own.

How VPNs Protect Your Data and Privacy

VPNs provide a number of benefits to ensure that your data remains private and secure:

1. **Encryption**:
   - One of the primary features of a VPN is **encryption**. When you connect to a VPN, your internet traffic is encrypted, which means that anyone who intercepts your data (such as hackers or even your ISP) won't be able to read it.
   - This encryption is typically done using protocols such as **AES (Advanced Encryption Standard)**, which provides strong protection against unauthorized access.

2. **Hiding Your IP Address**:
   - A VPN masks your **IP address** by routing your internet traffic through a VPN server. This makes it appear as though your online activities are originating from the VPN server's IP address, not your own.
   - By hiding your IP address, VPNs protect your identity and location, making it more difficult for websites, advertisers, or cybercriminals to track your activities.

3. **Secure Connections on Public Networks**:

- o Public Wi-Fi networks, like those found in cafes, airports, and hotels, are notorious for being **unsafe**. Without encryption, any data you send or receive can potentially be intercepted by hackers using tools to monitor the network. A VPN protects your data on these unsecured networks by encrypting it, preventing eavesdropping.

4. **Bypassing Geo-Restrictions**:
   - o VPNs allow you to access websites and content that may be restricted or blocked based on your geographic location. By connecting to a VPN server in a different country, you can make it appear as though you're browsing from that location, bypassing local restrictions or censorship.

5. **Bypassing ISP Throttling**:
   - o Some ISPs intentionally slow down your internet connection based on your usage patterns (for example, when streaming or gaming). With a VPN, your ISP can no longer monitor your traffic, making it harder for them to throttle your connection.

6. **Avoiding Surveillance**:
   - o VPNs prevent third parties, such as government agencies or advertisers, from tracking your online activities. This is especially important for

maintaining privacy when browsing sensitive information or accessing restricted services.

Real-World Example: Using a VPN to Access Region-Restricted Content

Let's look at a **real-world example** of how a VPN can be used to access region-restricted content, like streaming videos from a service that's only available in certain countries.

1. **Step 1: Accessing Content Without a VPN**
   o You want to watch a movie on **Netflix**, but it's only available in the United States. If you're in a different country (e.g., Canada, the UK, or Australia), the content is **geo-restricted** and unavailable to you. You receive a message saying that the movie is not available in your region.

2. **Step 2: Turning on the VPN**
   o You decide to use a VPN to access the content. First, you install a reliable VPN app on your device (laptop, smartphone, etc.) and launch the app. After logging in, you select a **VPN server** located in the United States (where the movie is available).

3. **Step 3: Connecting to the VPN**

   o The VPN establishes a secure, encrypted connection to the server in the United States. Your internet traffic is now routed through this server, and your IP address is replaced with that of the server, making it appear as though you're browsing from the U.S.

4. **Step 4: Accessing the Restricted Content**

   o You return to the Netflix website or app, and since your IP address now shows a U.S. location, the service thinks you're accessing it from within the country. The content that was previously unavailable to you is now visible, and you can start watching the movie.

5. **Step 5: Enjoying the Benefits of VPN Security**

   o Throughout the process, your internet traffic is encrypted, keeping your online activities private and secure. The VPN also prevents third parties from tracking your browsing habits and ensures that your connection remains protected, even on potentially insecure networks.

Summary

In this chapter, we've covered how **VPNs** provide a secure and private connection by encrypting your data and hiding your IP address. VPNs are essential for ensuring privacy when browsing the internet, especially on public Wi-Fi networks, and they help bypass regional restrictions or censorship. The **real-world example** of using a VPN to access **region-restricted content** illustrates how VPNs enable users to access services that would otherwise be blocked based on geographic location.

Whether for privacy, security, or accessing global content, VPNs are powerful tools that safeguard your online experience.

CHAPTER 20

THE INTERNET OF THINGS (IOT)

How IoT Devices Connect to the Network

The **Internet of Things (IoT)** refers to the network of **physical devices** embedded with sensors, software, and other technologies that enable them to collect and exchange data over the internet. These devices, ranging from home appliances and wearable devices to industrial machinery, can connect to the network to share information and receive instructions.

IoT devices typically connect to the network in the following ways:

1. **Wi-Fi**:
   - **Wi-Fi** is the most common way for IoT devices to connect to the internet, especially in **smart homes**. Wi-Fi provides a reliable and widely available network connection, offering high-speed internet access without the need for additional wiring or specialized equipment.
   - IoT devices such as **smart thermostats**, **smart speakers**, and **security cameras** often use Wi-Fi to connect to a home or office network, allowing

them to communicate with other devices or cloud services over the internet.

2. **Bluetooth**:

   o **Bluetooth** is a short-range wireless technology used to connect IoT devices over shorter distances. It's commonly used in wearable devices, such as **smartwatches** and **fitness trackers**, as well as **smart home accessories** like **smart locks** or **speakers**.

   o Bluetooth Low Energy (**BLE**) is a variant that is designed to consume less power, making it ideal for devices that need to operate on battery power for extended periods, like **fitness trackers** or **smart home sensors**.

3. **Zigbee and Z-Wave**:

   o **Zigbee** and **Z-Wave** are other low-power, short-range wireless communication protocols used primarily for **smart home devices**.

   o These protocols are designed to create **mesh networks**, where devices can relay data to each other, extending the range of the network and making it more robust.

   o **Zigbee** is commonly used in smart lighting systems (e.g., Philips Hue) and home automation systems (e.g., smart locks, smart hubs), while **Z-**

Wave is frequently found in smart security systems and home automation devices.

4. **Cellular Networks**:

   o **Cellular networks** (e.g., 4G, 5G) are used for IoT devices that need to operate over large areas or are located in places without Wi-Fi or Bluetooth connectivity. Examples of such devices include **smart meters, fleet tracking** devices, and **remote healthcare equipment**.

   o Cellular IoT devices connect to the internet via the same mobile network that your phone uses, allowing them to send and receive data from anywhere with cellular coverage.

5. **Ethernet**:

   o While Wi-Fi is the preferred connection for most home IoT devices, **Ethernet** (wired internet connection) may be used in more **industrial IoT applications** or in locations where a stable, high-bandwidth connection is required. For example, **security cameras** in commercial buildings or **networked sensors** in factories may use Ethernet for reliable and continuous communication.

6. **LPWAN (Low Power Wide Area Network)**:

   o **LPWAN** is a type of wireless communication technology used for IoT devices that require long-range connectivity with minimal power consumption. Examples include **LoRaWAN** and **NB-IoT** (Narrowband IoT), which are used in agriculture, smart cities, and environmental monitoring systems where devices need to send small amounts of data over long distances without requiring frequent recharging.

Real-World Example: Smart Home Devices Communicating Over the Internet

Let's explore how various **smart home devices** communicate over the internet as part of an **IoT** ecosystem. These devices can be connected to the home network and controlled remotely via a smartphone or voice assistant.

1. **Step 1: Setting Up the Smart Home Network**
   o You start by setting up a **home Wi-Fi network** with a **router**. This router serves as the central hub for connecting all the devices in your smart home. You also install the necessary mobile apps on your smartphone to manage the devices (e.g., a smart light control app, a home security app).

2. **Step 2: Connecting IoT Devices to the Network**
   o You purchase **smart home devices** such as **smart bulbs**, a **smart thermostat**, **smart locks**, and a **smart speaker** (e.g., Amazon Echo or Google Home).

142

- o Each of these devices has built-in Wi-Fi or Bluetooth capability. For example, you connect the **smart thermostat** to your Wi-Fi network by following the app's setup instructions. The thermostat now communicates with the app on your smartphone and can be controlled remotely.

3. **Step 3: Communication Between Devices**
   - o The smart devices send and receive data over the Wi-Fi network. For example, when you change the temperature on your smartphone app, the thermostat receives the signal over Wi-Fi and adjusts the home temperature accordingly.
   - o **Smart speakers** like Amazon Echo use **voice recognition** to control other devices. You can say, "Alexa, turn off the living room lights," and Alexa sends a command over the network to the **smart light bulbs**, turning them off.

4. **Step 4: Integration and Automation**
   - o Many smart home devices can be **integrated** to work together. For example, when you leave the house, you might have a **geofencing rule** set up on your smartphone that triggers the smart thermostat to adjust the temperature and turn off the lights automatically. This is an example of **automation** made possible by the IoT network.

5. **Step 5: Remote Monitoring and Control**

o One of the key advantages of IoT devices is **remote control**. For example, you could be at work and realize you forgot to lock the front door. Using your smartphone, you can log into the smart lock app and lock the door remotely.

o Similarly, if you're on vacation, you can monitor security cameras via your phone and ensure everything is secure at home. These cameras are connected to the internet and continuously stream video to your smartphone or cloud storage.

6. **Step 6: Data Sharing and Cloud Services**

o Many IoT devices send data to **cloud servers** for storage and analysis. For example, your smart thermostat may collect data about your home's temperature patterns and upload it to the cloud. Over time, the thermostat might use this data to learn your preferences and optimize energy usage automatically.

o Similarly, smart security cameras can send footage to cloud storage, allowing you to access it remotely if you need to review past events.

Summary

In this chapter, we've explored how **IoT devices** connect to the network using a variety of technologies, including **Wi-Fi**, **Bluetooth**, **cellular networks**, and **LPWAN**. We've also looked at how **smart home devices** communicate over the internet, enabling features like remote control, automation, and data sharing. The real-world example of a **smart home network** highlights the role of IoT in everyday life, improving convenience, efficiency, and security. IoT is transforming how we interact with devices, and its growing presence in homes, businesses, and cities is making the world more connected and intelligent.

CHAPTER 21

NETWORK ADDRESS TRANSLATION (NAT)

What is NAT and Why is it Necessary?

Network Address Translation (NAT) is a networking technique used to map private, local IP addresses to a single public IP address. It allows multiple devices on a local network (such as a home or office network) to share one public-facing IP address when accessing the internet. NAT is a key component in modern networking because it helps manage limited IP address space, enhances security, and provides flexibility for managing internal networks.

Here's why NAT is necessary:

1. **Limited IPv4 Address Space**:
   - o The **IPv4** address space is limited, with only about 4.3 billion unique addresses available. As more devices are connected to the internet, the demand for IP addresses has greatly increased.
   - o **NAT** allows multiple devices within a local network (e.g., a home or company network) to use the same **public IP address** when communicating with the outside world, reducing

the need for a unique public IP address for every device.

2. **Security**:
   - o NAT provides an added layer of **security** by hiding the internal IP addresses of devices within a private network. When a device within the private network communicates with an external network (such as the internet), only the public IP address of the router (or gateway) is visible to external parties.
   - o This makes it more difficult for hackers to directly target specific devices within the local network, since they cannot see the private IP addresses of individual devices.

3. **IP Address Conservation**:
   - o NAT allows for more efficient use of **IP address space** by enabling many devices to share a single public IP address. This helps conserve the limited number of available IPv4 addresses.

How NAT Works

1. **Private vs Public IP Addresses**:
   - o **Private IP addresses** are used within a local network and are not routable on the public internet. These addresses are typically reserved

by the **Internet Assigned Numbers Authority (IANA)** for private use and include ranges like:

- **192.168.0.0 – 192.168.255.255**
- **10.0.0.0 – 10.255.255.255**
- **172.16.0.0 – 172.31.255.255**

o **Public IP addresses** are assigned to devices that are directly connected to the internet. These are globally unique and routable on the internet.

2. **Translation Process**:

o When a device within the private network (e.g., a computer with a private IP address) wants to access the internet, the **router (gateway)** with NAT enabled changes (or translates) the device's private IP address into the router's public IP address. This allows the external network to recognize the connection and respond appropriately.

o The router keeps a **translation table** to remember which internal device made each request. When the external server responds, the router uses this table to forward the response to the correct internal device.

3. **Types of NAT**:

o **Static NAT**: Maps one private IP address to one public IP address. This is used when a device needs a consistent, direct mapping to the public internet (e.g., a web server hosting a site).

- o **Dynamic NAT**: Maps private IP addresses to a pool of public IP addresses. The router selects an available public IP address from the pool for outgoing traffic.

- o **Port Address Translation (PAT)**: Also known as **overloading**, PAT allows multiple devices on a local network to share a single public IP address by differentiating between connections using unique **port numbers**. This is the most common form of NAT and is typically used in home routers.

Real-World Example: How Multiple Devices Share a Single Public IP Address

Imagine you have a home network with several devices, including a laptop, smartphone, and smart TV. All these devices need to access the internet, but you only have a **single public IP address** assigned by your Internet Service Provider (ISP). Here's how **NAT** makes this possible:

1. **Step 1: Assigning Private IP Addresses to Devices**

- o Your home router assigns **private IP addresses** to each device in your home network, such as:
    - Laptop: **192.168.1.2**
    - Smartphone: **192.168.1.3**
    - Smart TV: **192.168.1.4**
- o These private IP addresses are used within the local network and are not directly accessible from the outside world.

2. **Step 2: Sending Data from Devices**
- o When the **laptop** wants to access a website, it sends an **HTTP request** to the internet. This request is addressed to the laptop's private IP address (192.168.1.2), but since the website is on the internet, the laptop's private IP address cannot be used directly for routing.
- o The **router** with NAT enabled takes the laptop's request and changes its private IP address (192.168.1.2) to the **public IP address** (let's say **203.0.113.10**) of your router. The router also assigns a unique **port number** to track this specific connection.

3. **Step 3: Sending Data from the Internet**
- o The router forwards the HTTP request to the website, and the website sends a response back to **203.0.113.10**, the public IP address.

- o The router looks up the **port number** in its NAT table and forwards the response back to the correct device (the laptop) with the private IP address **192.168.1.2**.

4. **Step 4: Other Devices Sending Data**

   - o Now, your **smartphone** and **smart TV** also want to access the internet. Each device will send data to the router, which will also perform NAT translation for each device's private IP address. The router uses different **port numbers** for each device to differentiate the connections, allowing the devices to share the same public IP address.

   - o For example:
     - ▪ Smartphone request: **203.0.113.10:1001**
     - ▪ Smart TV request: **203.0.113.10:1002**

   - o The router uses these port numbers to keep track of which internal device the responses belong to.

5. **Step 5: Returning Data to Multiple Devices**

   - o When the responses come back from the internet, the router uses its NAT table to route the data to the correct device:
     - ▪ The response to the laptop (port 1001) goes to **192.168.1.2**.
     - ▪ The response to the smartphone (port 1002) goes to **192.168.1.3**.

- The response to the smart TV (port 1003) goes to **192.168.1.4**.

In this way, all your devices can share a single public IP address, even though they have different private IP addresses internally. NAT ensures that the data sent to the public IP address is routed correctly to each device using the port numbers.

Summary

In this chapter, we've explored **Network Address Translation (NAT)** and its role in enabling multiple devices to share a single public IP address. NAT is necessary to conserve the limited number of available IPv4 addresses and provide security by hiding private IP addresses from the public internet. We also examined the different types of NAT (static, dynamic, and PAT) and provided a **real-world example** of how multiple devices in a home network can access the internet using a single public IP address through the process of NAT. This allows for efficient use of IP addresses and secure communication between devices on private networks and the internet.

CHAPTER 22

QUALITY OF SERVICE (QOS)

What is QoS and How It Improves Network Performance?

Quality of Service (QoS) is a set of technologies and techniques used to manage and prioritize network traffic to ensure optimal performance, especially for critical applications that require a steady, uninterrupted flow of data. QoS helps to allocate bandwidth efficiently and prioritize network traffic, making sure that high-priority applications (like video calls, VoIP, or online gaming) receive the necessary resources to function smoothly, even when the network is under heavy load.

QoS is essential for maintaining good **user experience** on a network, especially in environments where multiple applications compete for the same bandwidth. Without QoS, network traffic may experience delays, jitter, or even packet loss, which can severely affect the performance of real-time applications.

Key Features of QoS:

1. **Traffic Prioritization**:

o QoS allows networks to prioritize traffic based on the type of application or data. For instance, real-time applications such as **video streaming** or **VoIP calls** are more sensitive to delays and require high priority over less time-sensitive traffic like **file downloads** or **email**.

2. **Bandwidth Allocation**:

o QoS ensures that there is enough bandwidth allocated to critical applications, even when other traffic is congesting the network. By reserving bandwidth for specific applications, the network can deliver consistent performance without interference.

3. **Packet Scheduling**:

o QoS can define rules for how packets are sent across the network. Traffic can be classified into **different queues**, and these queues can be processed at different rates, ensuring that high-priority traffic is handled first.

4. **Traffic Shaping and Policing**:

o **Traffic shaping** involves controlling the amount and rate of traffic entering the network. It smoothens bursts of traffic and ensures that data flows at a steady pace. **Traffic policing** refers to monitoring and enforcing traffic limits, often dropping packets that exceed the defined rate.

5. **Latency and Jitter Reduction**:

   o QoS helps reduce **latency** (the time delay between sending and receiving data) and **jitter** (variability in packet arrival times). These issues can severely affect applications that require real-time data transmission, like video calls or online gaming.

6. **Error Handling**:

   o QoS can also include error recovery mechanisms, ensuring that lost or corrupted packets are retransmitted, and minimizing the impact on high-priority traffic.

Real-World Example: Prioritizing Video Calls Over Downloads

Let's consider a scenario where you are working from home and using a **video calling application** like Zoom or Microsoft Teams. At the same time, you're downloading large files, and the network is becoming congested due to multiple devices using the same internet connection. In this case, **QoS** can help ensure that your video call experiences minimal disruptions despite the ongoing file download.

1. **Step 1: Network Traffic Without QoS**

- o Without QoS, the video call and the file download would compete for the same available bandwidth. If the download is large and data-heavy, it could take up most of the network resources, causing the video call to experience high **latency**, **jitter**, and **packet loss**. This could lead to choppy audio, frozen video, or even call disconnections.

2. **Step 2: Configuring QoS for Video Call Prioritization**

   - o With **QoS** configured, the router or network device can be set to **prioritize** real-time communication over other types of data. This means the video call data packets are given **higher priority** and are sent first, even if there's network congestion.

   - o For example, the router might classify traffic based on the type of application. It identifies the video call packets (e.g., from Zoom) and assigns them to a **high-priority queue**. In contrast, the file download packets are placed in a **lower-priority queue**.

3. **Step 3: Traffic Shaping and Bandwidth Allocation**

   - o The router allocates **enough bandwidth** to the video call, ensuring that the call is smooth and uninterrupted. At the same time, it allows the file download to continue but limits its speed, so it doesn't consume all the available bandwidth.

- o **Traffic shaping** could limit the download speed to, say, 2 Mbps, ensuring that there's always enough bandwidth for the video call to run without interference.

4. **Step 4: Real-Time Application Performance**

- o As a result, even though the file download is still taking place, the video call remains clear and stable. The network resources are **shared efficiently**, and the QoS configuration ensures that the **real-time application** (video calling) always gets the **necessary priority**.

- o In this setup, you can continue your video call without interruptions, while the file download happens in the background at a lower speed, without affecting the quality of your communication.

5. **Step 5: Improved User Experience**

- o With QoS in place, the experience is optimized for both tasks. The video call has minimal lag, jitter, and packet loss, while the file download completes in the background without negatively impacting your work. QoS effectively balances the network traffic, improving overall performance.

Summary

In this chapter, we've explored **Quality of Service (QoS)** and how it helps improve network performance by managing and prioritizing network traffic. QoS ensures that critical applications, such as **video calls**, **VoIP**, and **streaming services**, receive the necessary bandwidth and low latency, even when the network is under heavy load. We've also seen a **real-world example** of how QoS can prioritize video calls over file downloads, ensuring that important tasks are not disrupted by other less time-sensitive traffic. By implementing QoS, networks can operate more efficiently, providing an enhanced experience for both real-time applications and general network usage.

CHAPTER 23

NETWORK TROUBLESHOOTING

Common Network Issues and How to Fix Them

Network issues can be frustrating, especially when they interrupt your ability to connect to the internet or communicate with devices on a local network. Here are some of the most common network problems and troubleshooting steps to resolve them:

1. **Slow Internet Connection**:
   - **Possible Causes**: Network congestion, bandwidth throttling by your ISP, weak Wi-Fi signal, outdated hardware, or too many devices connected to the network.
   - **How to Fix**:
     - **Check for Network Congestion**: If multiple people are using the internet for streaming, gaming, or downloading large files, the available bandwidth may be shared among them. Try limiting the number of active devices or activities.
     - **Restart the Router**: Unplug the router, wait 10 seconds, and plug it back in. This

can help resolve temporary connectivity issues.

- **Check for Software or Device Issues**: Ensure that your device's network drivers and software are up to date. Running too many background applications can also affect speed.

- **Use a Wired Connection**: If you're on Wi-Fi, try connecting directly to the router with an Ethernet cable. Wired connections are generally faster and more stable.

- **Upgrade Your Router**: If your router is outdated or doesn't support newer standards (e.g., **Wi-Fi 5** or **Wi-Fi 6**), consider upgrading to improve speed and coverage.

2. **No Internet Access**:

  o **Possible Causes**: Incorrect settings, DNS issues, router problems, or ISP outages.

  o **How to Fix**:

    - **Check Your Wi-Fi Connection**: Ensure that your device is properly connected to the network. If you're using Wi-Fi, verify that you're on the correct network and have entered the correct password.

160

- **Restart Your Modem and Router**: Unplug both devices, wait 10-20 seconds, and plug them back in. This can often resolve connectivity issues.

- **Check Your IP Configuration**: Ensure your device is receiving a valid IP address from the router. You can check this by running the **ipconfig** command (on Windows) or **ifconfig** (on Mac/Linux).

- **Check DNS Settings**: If you can't access websites by name but can reach them using IP addresses, your DNS settings may be incorrect. Try changing your DNS server to a reliable public DNS service like **Google DNS** (8.8.8.8 and 8.8.4.4) or **Cloudflare DNS** (1.1.1.1).

3. **Wi-Fi Signal Issues**:

   o **Possible Causes**: Interference, too much distance from the router, or physical obstructions.

   o **How to Fix**:

      - **Change Wi-Fi Channels**: If your router is set to auto-select a channel, try manually changing it to avoid interference from nearby networks.

- **Reposition the Router**: Place the router in a central location, away from walls or large metal objects that could interfere with the signal.
- **Use a Wi-Fi Extender**: If your home or office is large and the Wi-Fi signal doesn't reach certain areas, consider using a **Wi-Fi extender** or a **mesh network** to boost coverage.

4. **Connection Drops Frequently**:
   - o **Possible Causes**: Interference, router overload, or incorrect settings.
   - o **How to Fix**:
     - **Change Router Channel/Frequency Band**: Switching between the 2.4 GHz and 5 GHz bands can help reduce interference.
     - **Update Firmware**: Ensure that your router's firmware is up to date. Manufacturers often release updates that fix bugs or improve performance.
     - **Check for Overloaded Network**: Too many devices connected to the network can cause drops. Limit the number of devices connected to the Wi-Fi and prioritize important ones.

5. **Unable to Connect to a Specific Website or Service**:

   o **Possible Causes**: DNS issues, website outages, or router settings.

   o **How to Fix**:

      ▪ **Clear Your DNS Cache**: Flush the DNS cache on your device to resolve issues caused by outdated DNS records.

      ▪ **Use a Different DNS Server**: Switch to a public DNS server like **Google DNS** or **Cloudflare DNS** if you're experiencing DNS issues.

      ▪ **Check Website Status**: Ensure that the website is not down. Use online tools like **Down For Everyone Or Just Me** to check if the site is available.

6. **Local Network Connectivity Issues**:

   o **Possible Causes**: Incorrect IP configuration, faulty cables, or router problems.

   o **How to Fix**:

      ▪ **Check Physical Connections**: Ensure all cables, especially Ethernet cables, are securely plugged in. If you're using Wi-Fi, ensure your device is connected to the right network.

- **Run Network Troubleshooter**: On Windows, run the built-in **Network Troubleshooter** tool to diagnose and fix common network problems.
- **Ping Test**: Use the **ping** command to check connectivity between devices on the network or to the internet. This can help identify where the connection fails.

Real-World Example: Diagnosing Why Your Internet Is Slow

Let's go through a real-world example of diagnosing a **slow internet connection** at home. Here's how to approach the issue:

1. **Step 1: Check the Speed with a Speed Test**
   o The first thing you should do is check your internet speed using an online tool like **Speedtest.net**. This will give you a baseline and help you understand if your actual speed matches what your ISP promised. If the speed is significantly lower than expected, it's time to troubleshoot.

2. **Step 2: Check for Network Congestion**
   o If multiple devices are connected to the internet and using bandwidth-intensive applications (like

164

streaming videos, gaming, or large downloads), the network may be congested. Try limiting the number of active devices or pause large downloads.

o   Disconnect devices that are not in use and check if the internet speed improves.

3. **Step 3: Restart Your Router**

o   If your router has been running for a while, restarting it can help resolve temporary issues. Unplug the router, wait 10 seconds, and plug it back in. Check the speed again after the router reboots.

4. **Step 4: Check for Interference**

o   If you're using Wi-Fi, check if there are any obstructions (like thick walls or metal objects) between the router and your device. Move closer to the router to see if the speed improves.

o   If there's interference from other nearby Wi-Fi networks, try changing the Wi-Fi channel or frequency band (e.g., switching from 2.4 GHz to 5 GHz).

5. **Step 5: Check for ISP Issues**

o   Sometimes, the issue might be with your **Internet Service Provider (ISP)**. Check if there are any outages or service issues in your area by visiting the ISP's website or calling customer support.

6. **Step 6: Run a Traceroute or Ping Test**

   o   Use the **traceroute** command to trace the path your internet traffic takes to reach a website. If the connection is slow at certain points along the path, this can indicate network congestion or issues beyond your control (like problems with your ISP's routing).

   o   You can also use **ping** to check if packet loss or high latency is occurring.

7. **Step 7: Update Firmware**

   o   Ensure that your router's firmware is up to date. Outdated firmware can cause performance issues and security vulnerabilities. Check the router's settings page for any available updates.

8. **Step 8: Contact Your ISP**

   o   If none of the above steps resolve the issue, it's time to contact your ISP. They may need to perform diagnostics on their end or check if there are any bandwidth throttling or technical issues causing the slowdown.

Summary

In this chapter, we covered the most common **network issues** and provided troubleshooting steps to fix them. From slow internet speeds and connectivity issues to Wi-Fi problems and device conflicts, knowing how to diagnose and resolve these issues can save you time and frustration. The **real-world example** of diagnosing slow internet showed you how to approach the problem systematically, starting from simple checks like speed tests and congestion management to more advanced techniques like traceroute and ping tests. With these troubleshooting techniques, you can identify and resolve most common network problems and improve your network's performance.

CHAPTER 24

CLOUD NETWORKING

How Cloud Computing Impacts Networking

Cloud computing has revolutionized the way businesses and individuals interact with data, applications, and services over the internet. The core concept of cloud computing involves using remote servers hosted on the internet to store, manage, and process data, instead of relying on local servers or personal devices. This shift has a significant impact on **networking**, affecting everything from **data transmission** to **network security**.

Here's how cloud computing impacts networking:

1. **Increased Reliance on the Internet**:
    o   **Cloud computing** relies heavily on internet connectivity. Instead of accessing software or storing data locally, users interact with applications and store data on cloud servers hosted in data centers that could be located anywhere around the world. This means that high-quality and stable internet connections are essential for accessing cloud services efficiently.

2. **Scalability**:

o One of the main advantages of cloud networking is its **scalability**. With cloud computing, businesses can quickly scale up or down their IT infrastructure to meet demand without having to purchase new physical hardware. Cloud service providers handle the scaling automatically, and the network must accommodate fluctuating levels of data traffic and resource consumption.

3. **Virtualization**:

o Cloud computing uses **virtualization** to create virtual instances of servers, storage, and other network devices. Virtual machines (VMs) are created and allocated based on demand, allowing businesses to run multiple applications and services on shared physical resources.

o Networking is responsible for providing seamless communication between these virtual machines, enabling them to interact with each other and the outside world, without the user necessarily being aware of the underlying hardware.

4. **Data Redundancy and Reliability**:

o Cloud service providers often replicate data across multiple servers and data centers to ensure high availability and redundancy. This ensures that if one server fails, the data is still accessible from other locations. Network performance,

169

therefore, needs to support data replication and load balancing across multiple locations.

5. **Network Security**:
   o Security is a critical consideration in cloud networking. Since cloud data is transmitted over the internet, it's vulnerable to threats like hacking, unauthorized access, and data breaches. Cloud providers implement **encryption, firewalls, multi-factor authentication (MFA),** and **virtual private networks (VPNs)** to ensure the security of data both in transit and at rest.
   o Additionally, businesses must implement **strong network access control policies** to manage which devices and users can access the cloud network and its resources.

6. **Content Delivery Networks (CDNs)**:
   o Cloud providers often use **CDNs** to deliver content quickly and efficiently to users across the globe. CDNs cache content (like images, videos, or static files) in multiple locations, ensuring that users can access this content from a server closest to them, thus reducing latency and improving download speeds.

7. **Multi-Cloud and Hybrid Cloud Networking**:
   o Many businesses use a combination of **private** and **public cloud services** (known as **hybrid**

clouds) or multiple cloud providers (**multi-cloud environments**). Networking plays a key role in enabling communication between these different cloud environments, ensuring seamless data flow and security between on-premises and cloud systems.

Real-World Example: Using Cloud Storage Services

Let's walk through a real-world example of how **cloud networking** impacts everyday use, focusing on **cloud storage services** (e.g., Google Drive, Dropbox, or OneDrive).

1. **Step 1: Uploading Files to the Cloud**
   - You decide to back up important documents by uploading them to a **cloud storage service** like **Google Drive**. You connect your device to the internet and use the cloud service's application (web-based or desktop) to select files for upload.
   - Once you click the upload button, your device sends the data over the **internet** to the **cloud storage provider's data center**. This data is transmitted over various networking protocols, often encrypted, to ensure security during the upload process.

2. **Step 2: Data Storage and Replication**

   o The cloud service provider stores the files on their servers, often distributed across multiple **data centers**. The network behind the cloud service handles the data replication process to ensure that your files are available even if one server or data center experiences downtime. This ensures that the files are always accessible.

3. **Step 3: Accessing Files from Different Devices**

   o Later, you want to access those files from your smartphone. You log in to your cloud storage account using the mobile app and download or view the files stored in the cloud.

   o Your device connects to the internet and requests the files. The **cloud storage network** determines the best server or data center to serve the request, often based on your geographical location to reduce latency and improve download speeds.

4. **Step 4: Synchronization and Data Updates**

   o Suppose you make changes to a document on your laptop. Once you save the changes, the updated file is uploaded to the cloud automatically, thanks to **synchronization**. The cloud storage service ensures that the most recent version of the document is available across all devices connected to your account.

o The network infrastructure behind the scenes synchronizes these changes across various devices, making sure the updated data is available in real-time.

5. **Step 5: Downloading and Sharing Files**

o You may want to share a document with a colleague. You generate a shareable link or invite them directly via email. The recipient clicks on the link, and the file is downloaded from the cloud storage service.

o Cloud storage services use **Content Delivery Networks (CDNs)** to serve the content quickly and efficiently, ensuring that files can be downloaded from the nearest server to the user's location, reducing download time and improving the overall user experience.

6. **Step 6: Security and Data Privacy**

o Throughout this process, your files are protected by **encryption**. When you upload or download files, the data is encrypted in transit to prevent interception. If the files are sensitive, the cloud provider may also encrypt the data while it is stored on their servers.

o The cloud service uses network security measures like **firewalls, MFA,** and **secure network access**

policies to ensure that only authorized users can access your files.

Summary

In this chapter, we've discussed how **cloud computing** impacts networking, from enabling scalable, secure, and efficient data storage and processing to ensuring high availability and minimizing latency. We explored the key aspects of cloud networking, including **data redundancy**, **security**, and **virtualization**. The **real-world example** of using **cloud storage services** demonstrated how cloud networking allows you to store, synchronize, and access data from multiple devices seamlessly, with the added benefits of security and performance optimization via **CDNs**. Cloud computing and networking have reshaped how data is managed and accessed, providing more flexibility and scalability for both individuals and businesses.

CHAPTER 25

SDN (SOFTWARE-DEFINED NETWORKING)

What is SDN?

Software-Defined Networking (SDN) is an innovative approach to network management that decouples the **control plane** from the **data plane**. Traditionally, network devices like routers and switches have both the control and data planes integrated, meaning they were responsible for both making decisions (control) and forwarding the data (data plane). SDN changes this by centralizing the control plane in a software-based controller, making it possible to programmatically control the flow of data across the network.

In SDN, the **control plane** is managed by a **centralized software controller** that communicates with network devices (such as switches and routers) via standardized protocols like **OpenFlow**. This allows network administrators to configure, monitor, and manage the network more flexibly and dynamically than traditional networking methods.

SDN is fundamentally different from traditional networking because it makes the network infrastructure programmable. With SDN, network administrators can manage and modify the behavior of the network quickly through software, without having to manually configure each network device.

How SDN Changes the Way Networks Are Managed

1. **Centralized Control**:
   - o In SDN, the control plane is centralized in the **SDN controller**, which serves as the brain of the network. The controller communicates with network devices (e.g., switches, routers) to direct data flow. This centralized control allows for more efficient management and monitoring of the network, as administrators can make changes in one place rather than configuring each device individually.

2. **Programmable Networks**:
   - o With SDN, network behavior can be modified through software. Administrators use the SDN controller to program the network, specifying how data should be routed, how bandwidth should be allocated, and how traffic should be prioritized.

o This programmability is key for **automation** and **flexibility**. For instance, changes can be made in response to traffic patterns, application needs, or network failures in real-time.

3. **Improved Network Management**:

   o Traditional networking requires manual configuration of individual routers and switches. In contrast, SDN simplifies network management by allowing network policies, security settings, and configurations to be pushed to the devices from a centralized controller.

   o This automation reduces human error, simplifies troubleshooting, and speeds up the deployment of new services or configurations.

4. **Dynamic and Scalable Networks**:

   o SDN enables networks to be more dynamic and scalable. As the needs of the network change, administrators can adjust resources or traffic flow to respond to increasing demand or to optimize performance. This flexibility allows for more efficient use of resources, and the network can be expanded or contracted as needed.

5. **Better Security**:

   o Since SDN provides a centralized view of the entire network, security policies can be applied consistently across the network from a single location. For example, SDN can automatically detect anomalies or breaches and apply security policies across the entire network, helping to mitigate risks quickly.

6. **Network Virtualization**:

   o SDN supports **network virtualization**, which allows the creation of multiple virtual networks on top of the physical infrastructure. Each virtual network can be customized and managed independently, allowing businesses to run separate networks for different purposes (e.g., for different departments or types of applications).

Real-World Example: Managing a Data Center Network with SDN

Imagine a large **data center** that houses multiple servers, storage systems, and networking equipment. The data center network supports thousands of devices and applications, each requiring different levels of traffic management, security, and resource allocation. Traditionally, network management in such a setting would require configuring each individual router and switch to handle the traffic flow. However, with **SDN**, this process becomes much more efficient and flexible.

Here's how SDN would be used in managing a data center network:

1. **Step 1: Centralized Network Management**
   o The data center's **SDN controller** acts as the central hub for managing the network. This controller is responsible for defining network policies and configurations, such as how traffic should be routed, how virtual networks should be set up, and how security measures should be enforced.

2. **Step 2: Network Configuration via Software**
   o Instead of manually configuring each network device (like routers and switches), the network administrator uses the **SDN controller** to define high-level network policies. For example, the controller might specify that all video conferencing traffic should be prioritized over general data traffic to ensure clear, uninterrupted communication.
   o The controller automatically pushes these policies to the network devices, ensuring that the entire data center network adheres to the desired configuration.

3. **Step 3: Dynamic Resource Allocation**

- o As new applications or services are deployed, the SDN controller can dynamically allocate resources to optimize the performance of the data center network. For example, if a new application requires more bandwidth, the SDN controller can adjust the network paths and bandwidth allocation in real-time to ensure that the application gets the necessary resources.

- o If the network experiences high demand or traffic congestion, the SDN controller can re-route traffic dynamically to ensure smooth performance.

4. **Step 4: Network Virtualization**

- o The data center may host multiple virtual networks (for example, separate networks for **development**, **testing**, and **production environments**). With SDN, these virtual networks can be created and managed independently of the physical hardware.

- o The **SDN controller** allows the network administrator to create isolated virtual networks that share the same physical infrastructure but have different policies for routing, security, and traffic management.

5. **Step 5: Enhanced Security**

o   The SDN controller can detect potential security threats or unusual traffic patterns across the entire network. For example, if the controller detects an unauthorized device attempting to access the network, it can immediately block that device's access and enforce security policies across the network to mitigate potential breaches.

o   SDN allows security measures to be applied consistently across the entire network, reducing vulnerabilities that could arise from inconsistencies in device configurations.

6. **Step 6: Simplified Troubleshooting**

o   With the centralized control of SDN, network administrators can quickly troubleshoot issues within the data center. They have a complete view of the network and can easily identify problems such as bottlenecks, failed connections, or misconfigured devices.

o   Since the network is software-defined, administrators can make changes or adjustments in real-time without having to manually configure each piece of hardware.

Summary

In this chapter, we explored **Software-Defined Networking (SDN)**, a powerful approach to network management that separates the control plane from the data plane, centralizing control in software. SDN provides **flexibility**, **scalability**, and **improved security**, allowing networks to be dynamically managed and optimized with software rather than manual configuration. We also examined a **real-world example** of managing a **data center network with SDN**, where the SDN controller enables dynamic resource allocation, network virtualization, enhanced security, and simplified troubleshooting. SDN is transforming the way networks are managed, offering greater efficiency, automation, and scalability for modern data centers and enterprise networks.

CHAPTER 26

NETWORKING IN BUSINESSES AND ENTERPRISES

How Large Companies Manage Their Networks

Managing a network in a large business or enterprise environment involves handling vast amounts of data traffic, ensuring security, maintaining uptime, and supporting various services across different departments. The complexity of managing networks in such environments requires strategic planning, advanced technologies, and robust network management tools.

Here are some key strategies large companies use to manage their networks:

1. **Network Architecture Design**:
   o **Hierarchical Network Design**: Most businesses design their networks in a hierarchical manner, which consists of three main layers:
      ▪ **Core Layer**: The backbone of the network that connects different parts of the organization, ensuring high-speed data transfer between devices.

183

- **Distribution Layer**: Manages the routing and filtering of data between the core layer and access layer, ensuring that data is properly allocated and distributed.
- **Access Layer**: Provides access to end-user devices, such as computers, printers, and phones.

    o This structure ensures scalability and reliability, allowing the network to expand as the company grows.

2. **Use of Virtualization**:

    o **Network Virtualization** allows businesses to segment their network into multiple virtual networks. This isolation helps in creating secure environments for different departments or functions while optimizing resources. Virtual LANs (VLANs) and virtual private networks (VPNs) are commonly used to create these isolated environments.

3. **Redundancy and High Availability**:

    o To ensure the network remains operational at all times, businesses implement **redundancy**. This means having multiple devices, links, and data centers to back up critical network components. For example, redundant power supplies, load

184

balancers, and failover mechanisms are used to prevent a single point of failure.

- o **High Availability (HA)** configurations are employed to make sure that in case of a failure, backup systems can take over, minimizing downtime.

4. **Security**:

- o Security is a top priority in business networks, especially since they handle sensitive data. Companies use **firewalls, intrusion detection systems (IDS), intrusion prevention systems (IPS)**, and **Virtual Private Networks (VPNs)** to protect their networks from external threats.
- o **Access control** and **network monitoring** are crucial for preventing unauthorized access and ensuring that only authorized employees have access to certain parts of the network.

5. **Cloud Integration**:

- o Many enterprises integrate **cloud computing** into their network infrastructure to scale efficiently and manage data. Cloud services allow for remote access, flexible storage, and enhanced collaboration between teams spread across different geographic locations.

6. **Network Monitoring and Management**:

o Businesses use advanced **network monitoring tools** to track network performance, detect issues in real-time, and optimize network traffic. These tools provide visibility into the network's health, bandwidth utilization, and potential bottlenecks, which helps in proactive maintenance.

o Network performance management platforms often utilize automated systems to predict traffic spikes and plan capacity expansion before issues arise.

7. **Quality of Service (QoS)**:

o In large networks, different applications have different priorities. For example, **VoIP** and **video conferencing** require low latency and high bandwidth. **QoS** is used to prioritize critical applications and ensure they receive sufficient network resources.

8. **Disaster Recovery**:

o Business networks are designed with disaster recovery in mind. This involves creating backup solutions, such as **off-site backups** and **cloud-based disaster recovery** plans, to ensure that data and services can be quickly restored in the event of a failure or natural disaster.

Real-World Example: Building a Secure and Scalable Network for a Corporation

Let's go through a real-world example of **building a secure and scalable network** for a large corporation. In this example, the company needs a network that can handle thousands of employees, offer remote access, ensure data security, and scale efficiently as the company grows.

1. **Step 1: Assessing the Company's Needs**
   o The first step in building a network for a large corporation is understanding the company's requirements. This involves identifying the number of employees, departments, remote workers, the amount of data the network needs to handle, and critical applications that need to run on the network.
   o The company's needs might include support for video conferencing, file sharing, access to cloud applications, high-speed data transfer, and secure communication channels.

2. **Step 2: Designing the Network Architecture**
   o The company opts for a **hierarchical network design**:
      ▪ **Core Layer**: This is the central part of the network where the most powerful

routers and switches are located. It connects different offices and departments across multiple floors and buildings. High-speed fiber-optic connections are used for data transfer between the core and distribution layers.

- **Distribution Layer**: This layer manages routing, switching, and filtering traffic between the core layer and the access layer. Redundant paths are included to ensure network resilience.

- **Access Layer**: This layer consists of devices that connect directly to end users. For instance, workstations, laptops, printers, and mobile devices. Switches and wireless access points (WAPs) provide access to these devices.

3. **Step 3: Implementing Network Security**

   o The company installs **firewalls** at the network perimeter to prevent unauthorized access from the outside world.

   o **Intrusion Detection/Prevention Systems (IDS/IPS)** are put in place to monitor for suspicious activity on the network.

- o **Virtual Private Networks (VPNs)** are implemented for employees working remotely to ensure secure access to internal resources.
- o **Network Access Control (NAC)** is used to enforce policies, ensuring that only authorized devices can connect to the network.

4. **Step 4: Ensuring Scalability and High Availability**

- o The network is designed to be **scalable**, so it can accommodate future growth. The company invests in **modular switches** and **routers** that can be easily upgraded as the network expands.
- o **Redundant links** and **data centers** are set up to ensure **high availability**. If one server or router fails, the traffic is automatically rerouted through another device without interrupting the services.
- o **Load balancers** are used to distribute traffic across multiple servers to avoid overloading any single server.

5. **Step 5: Configuring Quality of Service (QoS)**

- o The company uses **QoS** to prioritize mission-critical applications like video conferencing and VoIP over less important traffic such as file downloads or web browsing.
- o Bandwidth is allocated dynamically, ensuring that video calls or cloud applications don't suffer

from slow speeds or interruptions, even during peak usage times.

6. **Step 6: Setting Up Cloud Integration**

   o The company integrates cloud services for file storage, application hosting, and remote access. **Private cloud** solutions are used for sensitive data, while public cloud services are leveraged for scalability and backup.

   o **Cloud-based disaster recovery** solutions are implemented to protect company data in case of network outages or physical damage to on-premise equipment.

7. **Step 7: Continuous Monitoring and Troubleshooting**

   o Network monitoring tools are set up to track performance, detect potential issues, and ensure uptime. The monitoring software provides real-time alerts in case of network failures, bandwidth congestion, or security threats.

   o Regular **network audits** are conducted to ensure compliance with security policies and to identify areas for performance improvement.

8. **Step 8: Employee Training and Documentation**

   o To ensure the network operates efficiently, employees are trained on network security best practices, VPN usage, and efficient bandwidth usage.

o   Comprehensive **network documentation** is created to ensure smooth troubleshooting, configuration changes, and future upgrades.

Summary

In this chapter, we discussed how large businesses and enterprises manage their networks to ensure performance, security, scalability, and reliability. The key strategies include hierarchical network design, cloud integration, redundancy, and robust security measures. We also explored a **real-world example** of building a secure and scalable network for a corporation, demonstrating how network architecture, QoS, and monitoring tools are implemented to meet the company's growing demands. Effective network management is crucial for ensuring smooth operations, and SDN (Software-Defined Networking) can play a vital role in simplifying and automating these tasks.

CHAPTER 27

THE FUTURE OF NETWORKING

Emerging Trends: 5G, AI in Networking, and Beyond

The field of networking is evolving rapidly, driven by advances in technology that are reshaping how networks are built, managed, and used. Some of the most significant emerging trends in networking include **5G**, the integration of **AI (Artificial Intelligence)**, and the continued growth of **cloud networking** and **network automation**. Let's dive into these trends and explore how they are transforming the future of networking.

1. **5G Networks**:
   o **5G** is the next generation of **mobile networks**, offering significantly faster speeds, lower latency, and greater capacity than **4G**. While 4G networks revolutionized mobile internet by enabling things like video streaming and mobile apps, 5G will unlock new possibilities for **smart cities**, **autonomous vehicles**, and **massive IoT deployments**.
   o **Key Features of 5G**:
      ▪ **Higher Speeds**: 5G promises download speeds up to 100 times faster than 4G,

enabling real-time data transfer for high-bandwidth applications like 8K video streaming and augmented reality (AR).

- **Low Latency**: With latency as low as 1 millisecond, 5G networks will enable applications that require instant feedback, such as **autonomous vehicles** and **remote surgery**.

- **Massive IoT Connectivity**: 5G will support the connection of millions of IoT devices in a small area, making it ideal for **smart homes**, **smart cities**, and industrial automation.

2. **AI in Networking**:

   o **Artificial Intelligence (AI)** is becoming increasingly integrated into networking to enhance the management and optimization of network operations. AI-driven technologies like **machine learning (ML)** can help predict network traffic patterns, automate troubleshooting, and enhance security by detecting anomalies and responding to threats in real time.

   o **AI in Networking Applications**:

      - **Network Automation**: AI can automate routine tasks like network configuration,

193

monitoring, and troubleshooting, improving efficiency and reducing human error.

- **Traffic Optimization**: AI can optimize traffic flow by predicting usage patterns and adjusting network resources accordingly. For example, AI algorithms can detect network congestion and automatically reroute traffic to minimize delays.

- **Security**: AI can improve network security by identifying and responding to threats faster than traditional methods. Machine learning algorithms can detect unusual patterns in network traffic that may indicate a security breach, such as a **DDoS attack**, and respond to it in real-time.

3. **Edge Computing and Cloud Networking**:

   o As more devices become connected, there is a growing need to process data closer to where it is generated. **Edge computing** complements cloud computing by processing data at the "edge" of the network, closer to the devices that generate it. This reduces latency and ensures faster responses, especially for time-sensitive applications.

o With edge computing, data from IoT devices, smart cities, and industrial sensors can be processed locally, reducing the amount of data that needs to be sent to centralized cloud data centers. This is particularly useful for **autonomous vehicles**, **smart healthcare**, and **real-time analytics**.

4. **Network Slicing**:

o **Network slicing** is an emerging technology in 5G that allows operators to create multiple virtual networks within a single physical network. Each "slice" can be customized to meet the specific needs of different applications or industries.

o For example, one slice could be optimized for ultra-low latency for autonomous vehicles, while another slice could be optimized for high-throughput applications like video streaming. Network slicing provides flexibility and efficiency in managing different types of traffic and services.

5. **Quantum Networking (Future Outlook)**:

o **Quantum computing** is still in its infancy, but researchers are exploring how it can revolutionize networking. **Quantum networking** could lead to ultra-secure communication channels using **quantum key distribution (QKD)** and faster data transmission speeds, powered by quantum bits (qubits) instead of traditional bits.

o Although it's not widely adopted yet, quantum networking holds the potential to fundamentally change how we transmit data and secure communications, especially for sensitive information.

Real-World Example: How the Future of Networking Will Change Everyday Life

Let's explore how these emerging trends will impact **everyday life** in the near future:

1. **5G in Smart Cities**:
   o In the future, **5G networks** will enable the development of **smart cities**, where everything from streetlights to garbage bins is connected to the internet. These cities will use **sensors, IoT devices**, and **AI** to improve efficiency and quality of life.
   o For example, **traffic lights** in smart cities will be connected to the cloud and able to adjust in real-time based on traffic flow, reducing congestion

196

and improving traffic efficiency. **Self-driving cars** will communicate with 5G networks to share real-time information, such as road conditions or hazards, making transportation safer and more efficient.

- o **Public services**, such as waste management, will use IoT sensors to monitor garbage bins in real-time, automatically sending notifications to trucks when they need to be emptied, improving efficiency and reducing costs.

2. **AI-Driven Networks in Homes**:

- o **AI** will play a significant role in managing **home networks**. With smart homes becoming increasingly common, **AI-powered routers** will automatically prioritize bandwidth for time-sensitive applications like video calls or streaming, ensuring that **latency-sensitive devices** get the best performance.

- o **Voice assistants**, such as **Alexa**, **Google Assistant**, and **Siri**, will use AI to understand your preferences and optimize the operation of various devices. For instance, smart thermostats will adjust the temperature based on your daily routines, and smart lighting will change automatically based on the time of day or your activities.

197

o With **AI-powered security systems**, your home will be able to detect unusual activity and send real-time alerts. AI algorithms will also monitor your home network for potential **security breaches** and take preventive measures, such as blocking suspicious devices or traffic.

3. **5G for Remote Healthcare**:

o The integration of **5G** in healthcare will enable **telemedicine** and **remote surgeries**. With ultra-low latency and high-speed data transfer, doctors can perform surgeries on patients remotely, operating medical devices through **5G-connected networks**.

o Patients will be able to wear **health monitoring devices** that continuously send data to their healthcare providers in real-time, enabling better disease management and more proactive care.

o **AI-powered diagnostic tools** will analyze medical data from patients, helping doctors make more accurate diagnoses and treatment plans, all facilitated through fast and reliable 5G networks.

4. **Cloud Gaming and High-Quality Streaming**:

o **5G** will dramatically improve cloud gaming and streaming experiences. Instead of relying on local devices to process high-quality graphics, 5G will allow users to stream games or movies in **4K or**

8K resolution directly from the cloud with virtually no lag or buffering.

o **Gaming consoles** or **mobile devices** will offload all computational tasks to powerful cloud servers, and 5G will ensure the data is transmitted at extremely fast speeds, making the experience indistinguishable from playing on a local machine.

5. **Augmented Reality (AR) and Virtual Reality (VR):**

o **5G's low latency** and high bandwidth will make **AR** and **VR** experiences more immersive and accessible. For example, **AR** applications in retail could allow users to virtually try on clothes, preview furniture in their homes, or interact with virtual environments in real-time.

o **Remote work** and collaboration will be enhanced through **VR meetings** where employees, regardless of their location, can meet in virtual spaces, enabling a more dynamic and interactive work environment.

Summary

In this chapter, we explored some of the **emerging trends in networking**, including **5G, AI integration, cloud networking**, and **network slicing**. These technologies are set to redefine networking, bringing faster speeds, lower latency, and improved efficiency across industries. The **real-world examples** showed how these trends will change everyday life, from enabling **smart cities** and **AI-powered homes** to revolutionizing **remote healthcare** and **cloud gaming**. The future of networking will create more connected, efficient, and intelligent systems that will transform how we live, work, and interact with the world around us.

www.ingramcontent.com/pod-product-compliance
Lightning Source LLC
LaVergne TN
LVHW022343060326
832902LV00022B/4209